Airports

A Century of Architecture

Airports
A Century of Architecture

Hugh Pearman

HARRY N. ABRAMS, INC., PUBLISHERS

Picture research by Mary-Jane Gibson

Designed by Bark

Library of Congress Cataloging-in-Publication Data

Pearman, Hugh.
  Airports : a century of architecture / by Hugh Pearman.
      p. cm.
  Includes bibliographical references and index.
  ISBN 0—8109—5012—X (hardcover)
  1. Airport terminals. 2. Architecture, Modern—20th century. I. Title.

NA6300.P43 2004
725'.39'09045—dc22
                                2004004242

Copyright © 2004 Hugh Pearman
This book was designed and produced
by Laurence King Publishing Ltd, London

Printed and bound in China

10 9 8 7 6 5 4 3 2 1

ABRAMS

Harry N. Abrams, Inc.
100 Fifth Avenue
New York, N.Y. 10011
www.abramsbooks.com
Abrams is a subsidiary of

LA MARTINIÈRE
GROUPE

Pages 2—3: Kuala Lumpur International airport by Kisho Kurokawa

This page: Dulles International airport by Eero Saarinen

contents

introduction

We tend not to stop and look at airports. Perhaps we are in too much of a hurry. But maybe we should, because no other building type does so much or has developed so rapidly. The 20th century, like the 18th and 19th centuries, was largely defined by rapid advances in transport technology. The canal age gave way to the railway age, which in turn gave way to the century of the motor car and the plane. By the year 2000 the airport terminal had become, strategically, the most important building type in the world. Airports had come to symbolize progress, freedom, trade and the aspirations of their host nations on the international stage. After some years of stern utilitarianism, their architecture had come of age. Airports once more had a glamorous sheen to them, as they had in the 1920s and 1930s. But in the early years of the 21st century, things are much tougher and much more uncertain. The outlook is intriguing.

We have passed the centenary of the airport. The Wright Brothers' first successful powered flight, from a moveable launch rail on the sands of Kitty Hawk, North Carolina, on the eastern seaboard of the United States, was in 1903. The following year they moved hundreds of miles inland to be near their Midwestern home town of Dayton, Ohio.

Introduction   The Most Exciting Places On Earth

There they chose as their testing ground the cow pasture known as Huffman Prairie – later Wright Field – which was later to develop into a key American military base. This meadow already possessed the key characteristics of an aerodrome in those early years. Large sheds, which acted as hangars and offices, were set to the side of a broadly oval field, allowing take-off into the wind from any direction – although the cows had to be moved first. The first passenger flight took place here, in a modified Wright Flyer plane.

Ever since Louis Blériot crossed the Channel from France to England in a monoplane in 1909 – the first international flight – architects have been fascinated by the idea of accommodating the plane. Arguably the first real airports were assembled for Edwardian air shows: already, in these tented townships, the distinction between 'landside' where people arrived, and 'airside' where the planes dominated, was in place, together with the separation of public and staff, and of operational and maintenance facilities. Before World War One several speculative designs for civil airports were in existence. The war brought the necessary rapid technical advances in aeroplane design, converting bombers such as the Vickers Vimy and Farman Goliath, which allowed the emergence of the airline industry in the post-war years. Europe, especially Germany – with far-reaching consequences – led the way. America was curiously slow to adopt air travel, and this became a matter of concern to US economists in the inter-war years. The catch-up, however, was swift.

From then to now, airports have been through several phases of development, usually to do with achieving the optimum flow of getting people through the buildings and on to the planes. The shift from elitism towards mass tourism in the 1960s was one significant spur to development, especially in Europe. Another was the internal deregulation of the US airline industry in 1978, which allowed open competition between American carriers for the first time. This massively increased the take-up of American air travel. At the time of deregulation 70 per cent of the American population had never flown. By the end of the 20th century

Above America celebrates the rapid progress of flight between 1908 and 1928, from the Wright bi-plane to the 'modern' Tri-motor in this poster.

Opposite New York's La Guardia airport, shown here in 1956, was the culmination of inter-war airport thinking, designed for both flying boats and land aeroplanes.

Previous US Air Force planes queue to unload their cargo at Tempelhof airport in 1948 during the Berlin Airlift in Germany.

that percentage had decreased to 20 per cent. The upshot was a spate of mergers in the North American airline business, leading to a handful of powerful carriers choosing to concentrate their operations at major 'hub' airports, with a consequent big expansion of building activity. Switching between planes at Atlanta, Chicago, Cincinnati, Denver and other such hubs became the pattern until this, in turn, was disrupted by the arrival of the point-to-point, low-cost airline model, which had been pioneered by Southwest Airlines even before official deregulation in 1971, although it did not become a large operator until the 1980s. The low-cost, direct-flight approach was quickly adopted by other airlines in both America and Europe. Low-cost operations do not like big, expensive airports.

Recently, the emphasis has changed further and not just because of strict new security measures – previously largely absent for internal US flights – that now make switching flights at hubs an ordeal rather than a minor irritation. Speed of movement is no longer the priority. Passengers are held in airports far longer than they used to be. Passengers are now seen as a captive market for retailing, something that increased security also encourages. The landside malls of bigger airports are increasingly destinations in their own right, much used by people who do not necessarily fly at all. Distance from the city centre is not regarded as a drawback when people are used to driving some way to a conventional out-of-town mall. Although the circumstances are utterly different, there is a historical parallel here: the early airports attracted, and were designed for, large numbers of people who merely came to look.

Airport buildings are having to adapt rapidly as the airline business itself undergoes commercial paroxysms – the most visible aspect of which is the significant customer switch from high-cost, high-overhead, large national carriers to low-cost, low-overhead, small commercial rivals. The low-cost attitude has profound implications for the design of airport terminals, which are largely based on the assumption that passengers will spend, spend, spend. But how long term, how seismic is the shift to budget flying? Is it as great a change as the arrival of the charter holiday aircraft in the 1960s, which first brought air travel to the masses as part of the concept of the 'package holiday', in which flight, board and accommodation all came at one fixed price? If it is, the hegemony of the great international airport may be threatened by a swarm of basic regional rivals, a return to the patterns of the early days of aviation.

But the indications are that things may not turn out this way. Small budget carriers rapidly swallow other small budget carriers, thereby becoming larger, more unwieldy, more conventional businesses with more conventional price structures. Air fares will rise anyway as the initial incentive deals struck between provincial airports and budget carriers drop out of the equation or are blocked as a form of hidden subsidy. More tax will be levied, particularly as an encouragement to anti-pollution measures. The taxation of aviation fuel, desired by many, would have far-reaching consequences. And long-haul flights remain the preserve of relatively few airlines, although the most active names change from time to time, particularly in periods of overcapacity. Farewell, Pan Am and TWA. Welcome, for the time being, Delta, American, United and Virgin Atlantic. The industry prediction at the time of writing, with all such companies feeling the

Above Much early aviation consisted of scenic excursions rather than scheduled flights. This poster dating from 1931 shows Passy airfield in the French Alps.

Opposite After World War One, many bombers were converted to airliners such as the Vickers Vimy, as shown here loading Royal Mail and other goods in London.

pinch, is for yet another spate of closures and mergers, resulting in far fewer full-service network carriers, operating alongside the maturing budget carriers in a still more deregulated market. This will have its impact on the way terminals are organized. Where it is normal in the United States for an airline to run its own terminal, for instance, that model clearly cannot apply beyond the moment that the government finally removes its block on overseas carriers operating internal American routes.

We are at a moment of change for airports in other ways. Expansion and new-build plans are increasingly targeted by environmental protestors, while the anti-globalization movement becomes more vociferous. New runways in small, populous countries are fiercely resisted. The design of terminals has had to adjust to massively increased security screening procedures in the aftermath of the terrorist attacks of 11 September 2001. Confidence is shaken when, as happened at London's Heathrow airport in early 2003 in response to a terrorist security alert, tanks and armoured cars ring the airport and soldiers with machine-guns stroll through the concourses. That extreme response to a perceived threat reveals just how vital to a nation's economic and symbolic well-being its principal airport is. Time and again, the argument advanced by politicians and businesses in favour of more and bigger airports is economic. The country with the best airports wins trade: particularly high-value trade. But the deleterious side effects of increased capacity – the environmental impact of more flights into bigger airports, the effect on more local trade – are equally well known. How can the two sides of this argument be balanced?

Airport planning in the broadest sense was immediately affected by the downturn in global air traffic following the atrocity of 9/11, and to that was added another inhibiting factor: fear of the spread of disease. In 2003–4 air travel to the Far East was drastically curtailed following the discovery of the SARS virus, originating in Guangdong province, southern China. SARS proved to be not nearly so virulent as first thought and was contained within months, but the reaction to it was tellingly extreme. The world's economists, as much as the world's epidemiologists, anxiously await the next, more deadly viral strain. Even without such dramatic incidents, economic slow-downs and outright recessions always immediately hit the number and type of flights people are prepared to take. All these things affect the way airports are planned and built in the short and even medium term. They can even affect the long term, if politicians are sufficiently short-sighted. This happened with plans for London's new airport, intended to be built at Maplin Sands on the Thames estuary in the early 1970s. A downturn in passenger numbers in the aftermath of the oil-price crisis of that period led to the project being shelved, resulting in severe consequent congestion problems in the UK that still resonate today.

But long-term planning, stripped of these blips, always looks the same: greatly increased air travel, everywhere. As the market matures, the rate of passenger growth will slow, but industry forecasts still show an average growth of between 4–5 per cent a year up to 2020. In parts of the world opening up to aviation – in particular China – the growth rate is much higher. It is perfectly likely that, as the Airbus company predicts, global passenger traffic in 2020 will be two and a half times its 2000 volume, and much more evenly spread around the world than it is

Above An attendant sells cigarettes on a BEA London to Gibraltar flight in 1960.

Below Preparations are under way at this flight kitchen in Albuquerque, US.

Opposite above A passenger lounge area at Albuquerque airport shows how it has adopted a pueblo-ranch style in its interiors.

Opposite below Style is as much a part of the experience of travel as flying – a check-in desk at London Gatwick in the 1960s shows the outfits of the time.

at present. Airbus obviously has a vested interest in selling planes, but it points to history: air transport has always shown a pattern of strong growth interrupted by a series of short-term downturns from which traffic has invariably rebounded to resume its growth trend (see, however, the conclusion to this book, Endnote on page 234, which sets out other prognoses).

So what should the buildings that serve this industry be like? Airports have the potential to be the most exciting places on earth. They offer architects the chance to design on the grand scale, in a manner not seen since the layout of new administrative capitals, from Canberra to Brasilia, in the 20th century. A large international airport expansion project typically costs from £1.5 billion to £4 billion ($2 to $6 billion) at the time of writing, and an entirely new airport of comparable scale double that. Even a small regional airport such as Eugene, Oregon in the US – a pleasing place of undulating timber beams with a mere 623,560 passenger movements in 2002 – has expansion plans costed at $62 million by 2017. The larger airports are now close to being complete, self-contained towns and cities, employing 100,000 or more with a population of twice that, virtually independent of the nations that host them. Like all cities, they never stay in a fixed form for long: successful airports must exist in a constant state of change as they adapt to changing circumstances.

Consequently, designing an airport is much more than a matter of designing buildings. It is a matter of designing a city-state, which has distant echoes of utopian thinking about it but which always carries the risk of turning into a dystopia instead. One thinks of Rex Warner's novel *The Aerodrome* (1941), a parable about the rise of a tyrant who takes over civilized society, here represented by an old-fashioned English village threatened and soon absorbed by the nearby military airfield with its complement of emotionless, power-hungry Übermenschen. When Warner was writing airports were still relatively small places (and still mostly fields), which meant that city airports could be relatively close to the centre, as was the case with New York's La Guardia, Berlin's Tempelhof, and Paris's Le Bourget. London's Hendon, and later Croydon, were a little further flung, though still close by today's standards.

Were Warner to write his allegory today, he would find rich source material in the form of vast airports placed many miles from the cities they serve, in some cases built on artificial islands or set in tropical jungles. Such places, with their own aerial supply routes and security systems, could simultaneously withstand a siege and topple a government. This is why, in a war, the airport is always one of the first places to be seized. It is why extreme measures are sometimes taken to prevent them and the flight paths into and out of them from becoming terrorist targets. An airport means more than trade. It means power and constant anxiety. Consider them, nowadays, as modern versions of the medieval fortified seaport, which had to handle large volumes of trade and throughput of strangers, while simultaneously defending itself from bellicose neighbours.

So the challenges are huge, but the rewards are great. Airports come second only to art galleries and museums in the pantheon of projects that the world's greatest architects most aspire to. Kansai, Kuala Lumpur, Hong Kong, Seoul, Paris, Chicago, San Francisco: the airports in these places are landmark

All pictures Saarinen's Dulles
International airport for Washington,
D.C. (1958–62) was the first to be
purpose-designed for jet travel.

structures as much as any Getty or Guggenheim. In 2003 architect Frank Gehry,
with a huge international reputation for creating cultural buildings, admitted that
there was one building type he would like to tackle on his own: an airport.

In the 1950s Gehry had worked with William Pereira on Los Angeles airport,
which was famous for its curvilinear restaurant on stilts, the Theme Building,
inspired by the film *The War of the Worlds* (1953). 'I got intrigued by the
impossible complexity of it,' said Gehry, and he continued: 'It was before Saarinen
had done Dulles. We were struggling with how to get the cars in and out, how to
get the people from the cars, how to get the baggage through – and it seemed
so complicated. Then all of a sudden Saarinen did this very simple thing and blew
us all out of the water. And now years later their solution makes less sense and
we're back where we were. The whole dynamic of the airport gets more and
more complicated, especially with security. That kind of complexity fascinates me
because you can try and find beauty in it. And because it's harder to do.'

That is the crux of the matter. Saarinen's 'very simple thing' was Dulles
International airport for Washington, D.C., the first airport designed specifically for
jets in 1958–62. It was a single large and graceful structure, a big roof under
which everything could happen. He clarified what had become a mess, but he
was working in more innocent times, when all passengers had to do was turn up
and take off. Complexity and mess were soon to creep back. At a casual glance,
today's airport terminals are, like Dulles, simply great big sheds – huge spaces in
which people meander around and which are more or less elegant and dramatic
according to the predilections of the architects chosen to design them. One
might be tempted to conclude that all an architect has to do is make big,
containing shapes. The truth is different. Airport terminals are hybrids, part
transport interchange, part factory, part distribution centre, part shopping mall.
They are a curious mix of the dynamic and the static. People rush to get there by
whatever means, then find themselves marooned for an hour or more in limbo,
then rush off somewhere else on a plane. In the meantime, exceptionally
sophisticated mechanical systems have processed people and baggage through
separate channels, while other systems have cleaned, maintained and
replenished planes and handled their staff.

It is a just-in-time system, all working towards the official carefully calculated
departure slot. Which is why, when delays occur, the knock-on effect throughout
an airport – and onwards into the surrounding airspace – is considerable. It is
said that the whole air traffic system of the United States can be flung into
disarray by problems at one crucial hub airport such as Atlanta or Denver. For this
reason Denver – one of the first of the new generation of airports built in
1989–95 and very influential on all airport designs since – was designed for
massive sequential expansion to keep up with rising demand for air travel.

In the face of such colossal logistical problems, it is all too easy for an airport
to become engulfed by its own engineering and for a new complex to be built as
a package by some international design-and-build contractor. Such arrangements
may provide all the facilities and space required, but at a different sort of cost. It
is difficult to quantify what is needed beyond the merely pragmatic because it is
intangible and thus not susceptible to actuarial calculation. But airports have
always been about much more than the simple processing of people from land to
air. Enormous technical ability is, of course, required for all the functional aspects

of an airport, but we notice those only if they happen to fail. In contrast, we are keenly aware of the architectural aspects. The appearance, the feel of the building and how it relates to the planes. The parts, in other words, with which we come into contact.

It is commonplace to compare today's best airports with the best of the great glass-and-iron European train sheds of the 19th century, but that view really describes only the genealogy of large-span, high-tech transport spaces. The European, specifically British model – to mix people and trains in one huge space – cannot apply to airports, for obvious reasons. A more apt train-plane analogy would be with a station that clearly differentiates its functions and has no such dramatic all-enveloping canopy. An airport should aspire to be today's equivalent of the 1913 Grand Central Station (see page 84) in New York or the original vanished 1910 Penn Station in the same city – places that dignified and exalted the whole idea of travel while acting as urban social focuses in their own right. Both these stations put the emphasis on the public areas – the shops, the restaurants, the gathering places. As the architectural historian Vincent Scully remarked of the old Penn: 'You entered the city like a God.'

At Grand Central today – and Penn was similar – visitors are scarcely aware of the trains, which are accessed via narrow portals leading down to tracks below, in principle not unlike the airbridges to planes. Other great east coast American stations, such as Philadelphia, make the same crucial separation of grand, uplifting architecture and actual point of departure, which is allowed to be prosaic. In contrast, London's historic Paddington Station, by Isambard Kingdom Brunel, Matthew Digby Wyatt and Owen Jones, was always conceived as the point of departure for an eventual transatlantic crossing from Bristol and was designed with an engineer's love of the machines that served it, with passengers and trains mingling at the same level. It is highly appropriate, then, that Paddington was later adapted to serve in part as a central London terminal for Heathrow airport, complete with rapid rail link.

There is, however, one crucial difference between such ancestral transport nodes and today's airports: longevity, or the lack of it. While Paddington lasted and adapted, the old Penn Station, which took 13 years to build, lasted scarcely more than half a century before redevelopment in Manhattan saw it toppled. The rate of change at airports is exponentially higher. The architecture of such places calls into question the whole matter of permanent versus temporary. The internal scenography of a terminal is liable to constant change, particularly in the retail sections. Forever struggling to catch up with demand and with changing requirements, all large airports are to a greater or lesser extent construction sites as new buildings are pieced into the overall complex and old ones overhauled.

The planes, plugged umbilically into the buildings or standing in solitary splendour just outside, are as valid a part of the airport's architecture as any of these buildings. They are also, in some ways, more permanent. The Boeing 747, to name the ubiquitous international airliner, has been a familiar feature of the world's airports since 1970. The Boeing 737, to take the canonic short-haul plane beloved of low-cost airlines and the most successful commercial aeroplane in history, has been around since 1968. Its appearance is older still, since its fuselage and nose derive from the Boeing 707 of 1950s vintage. Airliners, then,

Below Aviation became a passion for well-heeled women of the inter-war years. This image is taken from the cover of *Femina*, a French fashion magazine, dated 1931.

Opposite Europe's wig is being blown away by air travel in this poster dating from 1935.

through constant development, are long-lived beasts. Over that timescale, few parts of any major airport have retained much of their original appearance. Ergo, the plane is the real architecture: it might move, but it is always there. The building is the ephemeral object: it does not move, but its life is usually short and its appearance is more likely to be radically altered than that of the vehicles it serves. The architects of today's airport buildings are often celebrated, from Eero Saarinen to Renzo Piano, Richard Rogers to Norman Foster, Skidmore, Owings and Merrill (SOM) to Helmut Jahn and Kisho Kurakawa to Ricardo Bofill, but it is more rare to regard a designer such as Joseph F. Sutter, creator of the 747, as an architect. For Norman Foster, he certainly is. In 1991 Foster said of the 747: 'With about three thousand square feet of floor space, fifteen lavatories, three kitchens and a capacity for up to three hundred and seventy-seven guests, this is surely a true building … the fact that we call this an aeroplane rather than a building – or engineering rather than architecture – is really a historical hangover because for me, much of what we have here is genuinely architectural both in its design and its thinking.'

Foster points out that the only reason the 747 has lasted and will last longer than many buildings – a 50-year overall lifespan for the type is quite likely – is that it responds to change. In that, we can add, it resembles Brunel's Paddington Station. But whether one regards the true architecture as being rooted to the ground or about to take to the skies, a sense of equilibrium is beginning to emerge. The frantic airport building of recent years has slowed somewhat in the West, and though the emerging market of the Far East is still animatedly planning and building, particularly in China and Southeast Asia, the typology is accepted and Western architects and engineers are largely responsible for the expansion, though this will certainly change as China gains valuable expertise. America is well under way with its airport improvement programme, as typified by Atlanta Hartsfield and the new facilities at Kennedy, New York and Dulles, Washington – though plenty of squeeze points remain, many more new runways and their associated facilities are needed. In Europe, only Berlin-Brandenburg now stands out as a much-needed wholly new airport for a capital city, intended to replace Berlin's three existing small airports of Tegel, Tempelhof and Schönefeld. Athens had its all-new airport in time for the Olympics of 2004, a place architecturally anodyne to the point of ugliness, but at any rate of sufficient capacity, and in time. At the time of going to press Paris and London were talking of new main airports – the need being rather more pressing at London than in Paris – but in the meantime large-scale expansion schemes at London Heathrow and Paris Roissy (Charles de Gaulle) were keeping pace with traffic, as were similar schemes at Amsterdam's Schipol and Zurich in Switzerland.

As this build-out progressed and a breathing point was reached when global air traffic numbers temporarily declined, a fair degree of certainty became apparent about the future of the vehicles that these airports would handle. The last great oddity of commercial aviation, Concorde, ceased its regular scheduled supersonic services in October 2003. British Airways and Air France retired the 30-year-old planes in the face of mounting maintenance costs and public opinion that – after a fatal crash in France in 2001 – was coming to regard these

beautiful planes as unsafe. Unlike the 747, they had not been developed or improved: these planes were the entire original short production run, kept flying with periodic refits. There are no serious plans at the time of writing for a replacement supersonic airliner, nor – at the other end of the speed scale – for commercial airships, even in the freight sector. The Cargolifter Company, for which a giant hangar was built in Germany, became insolvent in 2002. Helicopter passenger services are confined to short-hop fringe locations, and other vertical take-off passenger craft are non-existent. Compared to the 1930s, then, when the designers of airports had to consider the rival merits of craft of all kinds, including airships, airliners and flying boats, matters are now straightforward. An airport must be able to handle various sizes of fixed-wing subsonic craft, with wheels, made by very few manufacturers – in the long-haul market, only two. That is a given.

It was not so long ago that things looked very different. As recently as 1999, when Kisho Kurakawa (b.1934) completed the first phase of his masterly Kuala Lumpur International airport in Malaysia, he wrote: 'Unquestionably, the world will have an entirely new high-speed transportation system by 2025 at the latest. This will be the HSST (Hypersonic Speed Transport), which will carry between 300 and 500 passengers at speeds up to Mach 3.5. The HSST will be meaningless for short routes. Therefore the required international hub airports will be limited to two in North America, one in Central and South America, one in Africa, two in Europe, one in Russia, and three in Asia.'

It is logical that such a new supersonic airliner will eventually be developed – attaining the speed is not a problem, only the acceptability, reliability and commercial viability of such craft – but one can only guess what its impact might be. Plans for regular services to fly even higher and faster than Concorde or the American Blackbird spy plane – effectively taking short hops into space, like ballistic missiles – tend to overlook the problem of the hugely greater cost of, and operational stress on, such vehicles, leading to a shorter operating life and thus a much shorter necessary payback period, and inevitably very high fares, so limiting demand in the first place. It took two wealthy European nations to build Concorde, and one global superpower (the old Soviet Union) to produce its short-lived Tupolev rival, while the United States, preferring to put a man on the moon, studied but abandoned the idea. The private sector cannot afford it, and a technological breakthrough of epic proportions would be required before it ever could. That is not impossible. In the meantime, the period to 2025, to take Kurokawa's suggested 'latest' date for the widespread adoption of such vehicles, is still a very long time in aviation terms. Which means that the current balance of airport and aircraft types is remarkably stable, just as trains and stations were for much of the 20th century, until significantly faster trains arrived towards its close.

In any event, an equation operates: given the huge costs that would be incurred by rebuilding the global infrastructure of airports to handle entirely new types of aircraft, any new airliner development now has to be exceedingly cautious. Today, airport design influences plane design as much as vice versa. It is hard to imagine a radically different airliner configuration – a flying-wing design, say, of the kind beloved of mid-20th-century designers such as Norman Bel Geddes – standing a chance today, when all the world's airports have long

Right The retirement of Concorde in 2003 meant that a reversal of history took place: ironically, the world had expanded again.

Below and opposite above The future of air travel in the post-Concorde era is represented by the giant subsonic Airbus A380.

Opposite below The huge doors of the CargoLifter Airshop Hangar in Brandenburg, Germany, were designed in 1997–98 and engineered by Arup.

All pictures The 747 was the first
plane to give considerable scope and
emphasis to interior design, which at
the time was unheard of since the
days of the airships.

been configured to disembark passengers from relatively narrow fuselages.
This constraint on plane design is comparatively recent. In the early days of
commercial aviation, the investment in buildings was not so great that unfettered
growth in plane dimensions was a significant problem: more huts could easily be
erected. Air travel was in any case so costly that only an elite indulged in it; mass
air travel really began to take hold only with the arrival of mass tourism. The size
and strength of the landing field was the key consideration then, hence the
eventual arrival, shortly before World War Two, of the permanent paved runway.
The 747 was the last great leap forward in airliner size, doubling capacity from
existing aircraft types.

This is why the double-decker Airbus A380, which has taken over from
Boeing's 747–400 as the world's largest aircraft, does not represent anything
like the radical step-change that the 747 did in the late 1960s. However, the
A380 pushes things as far as the great airports of the world will today allow. It
effectively covers an area of 80 x 80m (262 x 262ft), an appreciably larger
footprint than the 747, and all major airports are now planned around this
dimension and capacity. The last significant all-new international airport not to
anticipate an appreciably bigger airliner arriving was Japan's Kansai, built
between 1988 and 1994. The A380, starting with a passenger capacity of 555
but with a 'stretched' version of 650 seats also designed, is considerably wider
and heavier than its rival 747, even in its base model. That affects the design of
runways, taxiways and aprons, while terminals have to be designed to cope with
larger flows of passengers per plane, so affecting everything from the number of
check-in desks and security portals to the sizes of customs halls and the capacity
of the baggage-reclaim carousels. Even the relatively minor changes required by
the introduction of the A380 are expensive.

At Heathrow airport in London, a key European hub where four airlines were
expected to use the A380 straight away, the costs of adaptation were estimated
in 2003 at £400 million ($640 million) for modified taxiways to one runway, and
a significant upgrading of just one terminal and modest upgrades to another.
That money had to be spent to bridge a two-year period between 2006, when
the A380 was scheduled to enter service, and 2008, when Heathrow's
enormous new Terminal Five, designed with such large aircraft in mind, was due
to open. As many as 84 airports worldwide may eventually receive the A380.
While some of those will have anticipated the larger aircraft, many older ones will
have to make more radical alterations than Heathrow. The final global bill will be
large. Such are the associated costs of changing the industry-standard vehicle
even to this essentially modest extent.

It is worth noting also the other aspects of new construction demanded by a
new type of plane. Airbuses are put together from sub-assemblies made in
several European countries (in turn made from components sourced globally).
Previously these sub-assemblies – including complete wings and large sections
of fuselage, for instance – were transported around Europe by Airbus's Belugas,
the world's largest cargo aircraft. With the A380 that is no longer possible. No
economically feasible plane would be big enough to carry the bits. Instead, they
are transported by sea and land, so requiring large new docks, roads and depots.
The 'final assembly' building in Toulouse, France, where the sub-assemblies are

Above The LZ-129, known as the *Hindenburg*, and its associated hangars were an immense architecural presence over Lake Constance (der Bodensee), Germany.

Opposte above The recreation of the public lounge of the German airship *Hindenburg* is in the Zeppelin Museum, Friedrichshafen.

Opposite below A postcard of the *Hindenburg* dating from 1936.

brought together, is designed to produce up to eight new A380s a month. This is itself quite something: a building 500m long, 250m wide and 46m high (1,640 x 820 x 151ft) and covering 10 hectares (nearly 25 acres). That is a building longer than the Petronas Towers in Kuala Lumpur are high. It is a true groundscraper, but only the largest of many other A380-related manufacturing halls in France, Germany, Britain, Spain – and even a design office in Wichita, Kansas, USA. But the scale of the Toulouse Assembly Hall is such that it can immediately be placed in the same awe-inspiring category as the British, German and American airship hangars of the mid-20th century. A building where enormous planes are made must itself push technology to its limits. The roof sections of the Final Assembly Hall, for instance, each weighing 7,500 tonnes (7,380 tons), were assembled on the ground complete with all services and were then jacked 46m (151ft) into the air over the course of a day. This delivery of a large sub-assembly mimicked the assembly procedure of the planes themselves.

Boeing, which has a logistically simpler main manufacturing base in Seattle, USA, decided not to produce a newly designed A380 equivalent and also officially abandoned plans to further stretch its venerable 747. The world market for such ultra-large planes is relatively small (Boeing's calculations have it much smaller than Airbus's) and the main attraction to airlines is that fewer landing and departure slots are required, which at congested airports makes a big difference. The all-new A380 incorporates advanced construction technologies that are claimed to give it 15 to 20 per cent lower operating costs than a 747, and make it slightly faster. But instead of slugging it out head to head in this market, Boeing – having teased the world with its daring-looking delta-wing 'Sonic Cruiser' concept of a big, faster but still subsonic plane – has decided that the future instead lies with more refined conventional planes such as its 7E7, a medium-sized airliner designed to be as fast as the biggest existing planes at around Mach 0.85, but 20 per cent more fuel efficient. Air travel, it seems, is no longer about speed. As in the case of the railways a century ago, the system is in place and a generally accepted type of infrastructure and vehicle is – for the time being – universal. The technological challenge now is to achieve maximum efficiency – with a reduced ecological impact – while competing in other ways.

The interiors of the A380, in which London-based designers Priestman Goode were much involved, were market tested to exhaustion and were the most architectural aircraft interiors yet, complete with lounges, bars and grand staircases. The stated aim was to make more space. But only up to a point: in A380 economy class the seat pitch was designed to remain at an industry standard of 81–84cm (32–33in) – but perhaps a little wider than previously, because travellers are getting fatter. Given public concern at the time of the plane's design – that prolonged air travel in cramped conditions is very bad for people's health, particularly leading to the condition known as deep-vein thrombosis (DVT) – it will be interesting to see how various airlines make use of the extra fuselage space at their disposal.

Parts of the A380 interiors (as envisaged by Airbus rather than the operators) are designed to resemble, not so much aircraft, as the business-class lounges to be found at all the world's big airports. Once again, the architecture of flight and the architecture of terra firma are coming together. We see this happening also at the £2.5 ($3.5) billion expansion of Dubai airport, where the architecture of the top deck of the Emirates Airline's A380s – in their case entirely given over to

premium-class passengers – is matched by the architecture of the top deck of the new terminal buildings, where the lounges are also for the sole use of premium-fare passengers, who board their planes directly at this level. Thus the design of the plane and the design of the terminal were considered as one. It is interesting to see that as with many Victorian and Edwardian theatres, upper deck means upper class. This is not how Airbus itself envisaged the seating layout of its plane, which was as a mix of classes on both levels, but the fact is that the architecture of the plane can accommodate such differences – purely by being two storeys.

Many lavish interior design studies, some not so dissimilar in approach to Airbus's own A380 exercises, were also carried out during the original development of the 747 in the 1960s. Few made it into the air, and one reason for this, as given by some operators taking delivery of the A380, is that they feel they must offer roughly the same standard of accommodation across all their long-haul planes. If one type of plane is notably better, that will affect the commercial viability of the rest of their fleets. So there is less scope for innovation than might at first appear. Not since the days of the Zeppelins, the big

Short and Curtiss flying boats, and the fat-bellied post-war Boeing Stratocruisers, have airlines offered real space as their key product for the majority of their passengers. Even then, a class system operated. And tellingly, those were the days when air travel was very expensive. Today, just as when ocean-going ships were the principal means of intercontinental travel, it is possible to buy space only by paying premium fares. Economy fares mean economical dimensions.

One place where passengers of all classes and ticket types should be able to enjoy space is the airport terminal. But cheap, out-of-the-way terminals for budget airlines do not build much by way of facilities. Even airbridges to the planes are frequently eschewed on cost grounds. If better facilities are provided, the fees charged to the airlines are increased and the budget airlines either cease to be budget or go to a basic military airfield elsewhere. All this raises the question: what sort of airports will be needed over the next 20 to 50 years?

The trend towards steadily larger international airports was given a substantial fillip when the United States adopted its 'hub' system, which meant that hub airports handled an enormous number of passengers changing planes on the way to somewhere else, rather than making a single flight. This trend has continued in the Far East with such examples as Japan's Kansai, Hong Kong's Chek Lap Kok, Korea's Incheon, China's Beijing and Shanghai-Pudong, Malaysia's Kuala Lumpur, Singapore's Changi and Thailand's Bangkok. All these to some extent pull in their wake the need for a new breed of smaller regional airports, which double up with what used to be called 'commuter' airports for internal flights and short international hops. To which add the prospect of revived smaller regional airports, driven by the budget-flight operators. Periodically, when

Opposite Kansai airport, Japan, designed by Renzo Piano, is an example of a modern-day hub, which acts as a vast interchange for all types of travel.

capacity constraints at London Heathrow are reached, the possibility is discussed of Amsterdam's Schipol becoming effectively the international airport for southern England, with onward short-hop flights to London's Stansted, Birmingham or wherever. There is no reason, apart from national pride, for the relevant hub airport not to be in a convenient nearby country, just as in America it may be in the adjoining state. But this view ignores basic psychology. A traveller to a capital city – London, say – wants to fly straight to London. The solution, in the case of cities such as New York, Paris and London, is to cease to regard the various airports of those cities as separate, but instead to think of them as being simply the various terminals of one large city-wide airport. Of course, the infrastructure needed to make this approach work cleanly tends to drag behind: dedicated rapid rail links between the airports of a given city are not nearly so much in evidence as the transit systems between the terminals within each airport or between airports and the city centre.

The airport terminal is a building type that has had a century to develop. We have seen how it combines elements of several other building types of today. Its roots are more complex still, to be found in earlier building types, such as factories, botanical glasshouses, railway stations and shipyards, hotels and clubs, post and telegraph offices, department stores, even hospitals, military barracks and fortresses. Aspects of all these antecedents feed into the design of the airport terminal building, which can thus be read as an amalgam of architectural types. But one inevitably returns to the proposition that the airport as a whole is not really a building type at all. It is too dispersed and has to do too many things. It is, in effect, a town or city, requiring broad urbanistic skills as well as architectural, structural and mechanical expertise.

This book looks at how the airport has developed as a concept and a reality ever since humans first floated off the ground in the 18th century. Chapter 1 examines the origins of the airport in the early years of powered flight and the technological impetus provided by World War One. Chapter 2 recounts the birth and growth of civil aviation in the inter-war years and how the airport terminal evolved as a new type of building, especially in Europe. Chapter 3 takes a more sidelong look at things through the romantically misguided notions of several generations of visionary architects. Chapter 4 discusses the key metaphor of airport buildings from the 1930s to the present day – the imagery of flight. In Chapter 5 we see how the arrival of the jet age stimulated rapid expansion and a reconsideration of what an airport should be. It is not just a picture of endless sprawl: Chapter 6 reflects on the appeal of the smaller airport. With Chapter 7 we move on to the latest mega-airports of the world, those that can most truly claim to be cities in themselves. And in the Endnote we consider the future. Or rather, six different possible futures for this simultaneously exciting and exasperating phenomenon of our times.

The success of an airport is conventionally measured by its efficiency, by its ability to manage the arrival and departure of planes on time for the minimum of passenger effort. While much of this is to do with technically complex interlocking systems stretching internationally, the successful airport is about more than military precision. People spend a lot of time in these buildings, or merely pass through them on our way to somewhere else. Architecture is called upon to do many things here, but one of its principal tasks – even if this never appears in any briefing document – is to calm the nerves and lift the spirits. We have to feel confidence in our airport buildings, and more than that. Just as a great railway station never palls, so an airport terminal should provoke a sense of delight and pleasurable anticipation. It is not easy. But it is achievable.

chapter one

When was the first airport built? Huffman Prairie at Simms Station near the Wright Brothers' home town of Dayton, Ohio, has the strongest claim, given that it had a modest public face as well as a testing function, that the planes there flew relatively long distances, rather than merely hopping, and that pilots were trained there. This 34 hectare (84 acre) patch of damp cow pasture, with its timber hangars dating from 1904 and 1905, its boundary marker flagpoles and its launching derricks, is where the Wrights did their proving work, having returned from making the first flight far away at Kitty Hawk, North Carolina, with its usefully constant coastal winds.

Although the Wrights had built a basic hangar at Kitty Hawk in 1903, it was not a dedicated airfield and it served a temporary purpose only. It is, therefore, Huffman Prairie that must be regarded as the mother and father of today's airports and 1904 as its foundation date. After two years of testing there, the Wrights stopped flying for a while as they waited for the patent to come through on their plane. In the meantime they attempted to negotiate deals to sell planes and training packages to the US, British and French governments.

Chapter One   Origins

The prairie was very public, with a main road and tramway passing nearby, and after their initial enthusiasm for publicity the Wrights clearly became nervous that there might be industrial spies among the many visitors who came to see them fly. A lot of money was at stake: the first one-off Wright military plane sold for $30,000 in 1909, and by 1911, despite competition from the rival Curtiss company, the going rate for a production plane was still a healthy $5,000. Huffmann Prairie became the Wright Company School of Aviation from 1910 to 1916, and today it is preserved, complete with replica hangar, within the heart of the Wright-Patterson Air Force base. But the story did not quite begin there. Huffman Prairie had interesting precedents.

If we go back before the time of heavier-than-air craft, a case can be made for some of the facilities designed for 19th-century prototype airships. At Chalais-Meudon near Paris, for instance, engineers Charles Renard and Arthur Krebs successfully piloted the first navigable airship in 1884. Their development programme included a steel lattice-frame hangar, built in 1879, made from modular metal components and glazed panels left over from the 1878 Paris Expo. It is likely that these components were originally designed by Gustave Eiffel, who – if we stretch a point – can be said to have had a hand in the first building for powered flight.

Serious unbuilt designs go back a century further, to the French military engineer Jean-Baptiste-Marie Meusnier de la Place (1754–93), who designed a propeller-driven dirigible and a tent-like hangar to house it in 1784, very soon after the first balloon flights of the Montgolfier brothers. Meusnier never built either – he was killed in 1793 at the battle of Kassel – but we know the airship would have worked, because in 2002 a scaled-down replica version was built to his designs in Britain, under the direction of the structural engineer Professor Chris Wise, and successfully flown. Wars always stimulate developments in aviation, so it comes as no surprise to learn that Meusnier's was intended as a way of taking troops over enemy lines. It was an ambitious design, intended to carry 80 men, but it depended on hand-cranked propellers, which would have limited its range severely.

Above The Wright Brothers in May 1904, with their Flyer II at Huffman Prairie, Ohio, USA.

Right Meusnier's tent-like hangar for his planned airship, 1784: possibly the first lighter-than-air structure.

Opposite The first navigable airship's hangar, 1879, used components designed by Eiffel.

Previous Zeppelin LZ–6 in the floating shed at Friedrichshafen.

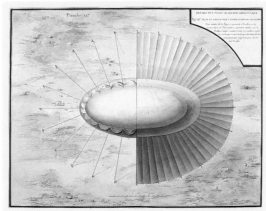

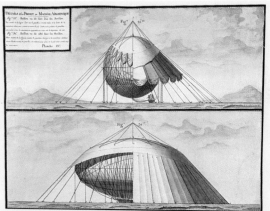

Above Graf von Zeppelin, shown
here in a 1908 poster, was a Prussian
soldier aristocrat as well as creator of
the engine-powered, steerable airship.

Below Zeppelins became a modish
shape – here one is used to advertise
a brewery in Berlin in 1925.

Opposite A postcard showing
Zeppelin's floating hangar at
Friedrichshafen on Lake Constance,
Germany, 1908, with airship LZ–4.

Then there is Germany. Proving that powered flight was not just a young man's
game, on 2 July 1900, when he was 62 years old, Ferdinand, Graf von Zeppelin,
the Prussian soldier and count, flew five passengers several miles at
considerable height – if somewhat unsteadily – in his first rigid airship, powered
by Daimler-Benz engines. Von Zeppelin (1838–1917) achieved a 24-hour flight
in 1906 when the Wrights were struggling to manage 40 minutes. His
Friedrichshafen base on the German side of Lake Constance can thus claim to
be the world's first passenger terminal – and it must have been an interesting
one, given that his airships emerged from a floating hangar on the lake. Airports
and water have always enjoyed a symbiotic relationship: initially because the air
currents over water were favourable and crashes more survivable; later because
flying boats could use existing harbours where land airports were yet to be built;
later still because take-off over water meant no obstructions and less noise for
land-dwellers; and finally because large airports could be built on reclaimed land
in the sea when land was scarce.

To understand the nature of the architecture that emerged to serve aviation,
we must first consider the nature of the beast itself: the powered flying machine.
Lighter-than-air craft, such as dirigibles and airships, have their own specific
requirements, as do flying boats and seaplanes, and these will take their place in
this narrative. But the airport of today serves the system that eventually won out
over these rivals – powered, wheeled, heavier-than-air machines requiring
considerable amounts of space both to manoeuvre on the ground and to leave
and return to terra firma. The history of these machines goes back rather further
than most people imagine. Leaving aside the many thinkers who imagined
manned flight from earliest time – thus leaving aside even Leonardo, who did not
attempt to build what he drew – brings us to the mid-19th century and Sir
George Cayley (1773–1857). This British pioneer of aeronautics, whose gliders
carried the first people ever to fly in heavier-than-air craft in 1849 and 1853,
was an impeccable scientist, whose breakthrough was to understand and
promote the principle of the fixed-wing craft as opposed to bird-like, flapping-
wing devices. But the fixed-wing format needs a particular kind of space to get
off the ground – level or facing downhill and into the wind. Cayley's designs were
incredibly advanced for their time, but one thing held him back. He correctly
predicted that true sustained powered flight would have to wait until a sufficiently
lightweight engine was developed.

Experiments continued throughout the 19th century around the world, but
especially in France, with the race being to find the smallest, lightest means of
propulsion. Steam engines were preferred, with compressed-air devices also
being popular. A number of these planes made short hops into the air, mostly
when launched downhill. Already the linear nature of the airfield was emerging.

It is possible to suggest, for instance, that the world's first 'airport' was built by
Sir Hiram Maxim (1840–1916), the American-born, British-nationalized inventor
of the machine-gun that bears his name. The biggest and most advanced
manned powered plane to 'fly' before the Wright Brothers' plane was his. This
twin-engined behemoth, 61m (200ft) long and with a wingspan of 33m (107ft),
had a crew of three and weighed 3,629kg (8,000lb) fully loaded. It was the result
of exhaustive research into aeronautics – Maxim used a whirligig and a wind

Above Edwardian airshows developed the airfield, often from racetrack origins. This poster, dating from 1922, advertises an International Week of Air Travel in Nice.

Opposite Sir Hiram Maxim's giant flying machine of 1893 required a large hangar, 550m (1,800ft) of launch tracks and a great deal of open space, ten years before the Wright Brothers were working.

tunnel – and lightweight steam engines and was successfully tested several times, starting in 1893. His 'airport' consisted of a large hangar in a field near Bexley in Kent, England, from which emerged twin rails extending for 550m (1,800ft). The rails not only guided the four-wheeled machine but also prevented it from rising too high in the air. After several successful launches, however, the machine was damaged when one of the restraining rails broke during a 'flight' at 68kph (46mph) and hit a propeller. It was 31 July 1894, and Maxim never 'flew' again. Did he lose his nerve? Whatever the reason, he abandoned his costly researches, content that he had proved that powered flight could be done, and moved on to other things. A giant propeller from this Victorian plane survives, and to this day there is an original Maxim-designed fairground ride at Blackpool Pleasure Beach in northwest England called 'Sir Hiram Maxim's Flying Machines'. People whirl round and round in gondolas held on chains, which was pretty much how he used to test the aerodynamics of his plane designs.

France, however, has a slightly earlier claim than Maxim, in the form of the experiments of the aviator Clément Ader (1841–1926) with his bat-like plane, the Eole. Ader's compact, alcohol-powered steam engine worked well, and in 1890 he made short powered hops from a level surface 200m (656ft) long, which we may regard as the precursor to the runway. As Maxim was to find, however, the real problem was not so much getting into the air, as knowing what to do once the plane was up there. How was it to be controlled? Backed by the French government, Ader made a bigger craft in 1897 that failed to rise into the air at all, although he was to spend most of his life claiming to have been the first man to fly a powered aircraft any distance. Official French government reports later set the record straight: he had not succeeded.

This brings our story back to America, still in the pre-Wright era. Government-funded experiments into powered flight by the distinguished astronomer and aeronauticist Samuel Pierpoint Langley (1834–1906) proved abortive. His early unmanned planes flew very well under power, but until 1903 his bigger manned versions collapsed on launching. This was because Langley avoided airfields, preferring to launch his planes (which he called 'aerodromes') over water with powerful catapults. The airframes could not handle the stress, nor had Langley (like Maxim and Ader) considered sufficiently how to manoeuvre the craft once airborne. Langley's launch technique is reminiscent of the German glider pioneer Otto Lilienthal (1848–96), who in 1894 made an artificial hillock with a circular shed on top to house his craft. From the roof of this shed, Lilienthal would leap and run, strapped into his gliders, and fly several hundred metres. Langley's related system – aircraft launched from the top of a building, in his case a large houseboat on the Potomac River – was to continue to have its adherents, especially among architects, as the 20th century progressed. The airport on the roof is a seductive concept, though it has only become useful for helicopters.

All these heavier-than-air forerunners to the Wrights' planes in America, Britain and France indicated the emerging form of the land-based facilities that powered planes would need: the hangar, the field, the rails or the prepared ground, all present and correct in late in Victorian times. So the modern airfield configuration was set when the Wright Brothers went the necessary final step on the sands of Kitty Hawk. Rather than going for size and brute power as Maxim had done, they

Below Zeppelins were running commercial passenger-carrying flights well before World War One. This 1915 poster advertises a Zeppelin in a German Bohemia Show.

Opposite above Huffman Prairie develops: the Wright Flyer III had a purposeful air and was the first production model in 1905.

Opposite below Aristocrats take to the skies: Wilbur Wright (right) shows off the Flyer to King Alfonso XIII of Spain at a Paris flying school, 1909.

took the opposite tack: extreme lightness of construction and a single, compact petrol engine of their own design. Where Ader, Maxim and Langley had been unsure how to control a plane once it was in the air, Wilbur and Orville Wright had worked that out, thanks to their system of 'wing warping', later replaced with ailerons, to allow their plane to bank and turn.

Once the first short flight had taken place, development was very rapid. Working from the pasture 13km (8 miles) east of Dayton that its owner Torrence Huffman, a local banker, allowed the Wright Brothers to use, the techniques of manned flight were established. Two years later the 1905 Wright Flyer III proved capable of sustained, even relatively high-level flight, and it is regarded as the world's first practical, fully tested aeroplane. Despite being first to produce a military plane, the Wrights gradually lost the initiative to rival plane makers such as America's Glenn Curtiss, who later specialized in seaplanes and flying boats, and France's Louis Blériot with his advanced monoplane, as well as to the British and German machines that came to dominate World War One. Orville Wright was left somewhat stranded by the death of his cleverer older brother Wilbur in 1912. He designed no successor to the temperamental Flyer, which was quickly out of date, and sold out of his company – which was to become famous for aero-engines rather than planes – in 1915. But by then the Huffman Prairie Flying Field, as it became known, had its place in history. All earlier inventors had places where they tried out their flying machines, but it was at Huffman Prairie that a consistently working aerodrome for heavier-than-air machines first emerged.

In the early days, with airships challenging aeroplanes, the buildings of an airfield were principally to house and maintain the fragile planes or dirigibles. Unlike today, the craft were not buildings in themselves that could be left out in the open for long periods, and airships were particularly vulnerable to side-winds. Having no dead weight to hold them to the ground, they had to be kept floating in huge hangars, the technology of which can be traced back to the large, covered ship-docks familiar throughout the world from the early 19th century, large-span spaces that mutated first into botanical glasshouses, then into railway sheds. Needing (like all aircraft) to set off into the wind, it became necessary to make these huge buildings rotatable. Von Zeppelin soon enclosed his floating pontoons and achieved his first floating airship hangar on Lake Constance in 1907. By 1910 he had land-based rotating sheds. The United States was later to adopt the technology of both the Zeppelin company and the rotating sheds – the largest of all being the Akron Airdock of 1929, with its huge clamshell doors.

In any event, the idea of the large-span building at an airfield was to prove useful. Early designs for an airport, such as Erich Mendelsohn's 1914 sketch for an aerodrome, created in his plastic, expressionist style, envisage a large central building (to house a dirigible) with ancillary buildings stretching to either side for fixed-wing planes. Remove the airship and reconsider the large central hall as a passenger terminal, and the layout of Mendelsohn's terminal building is not so very different from the layouts of most airport terminals of today. We shall see what this idea led to in the next chapter.

After Huffman Prairie, the model that influenced the evolution of the airport most – because of the huge numbers of people it was able to process – was the Edwardian, or *belle époque*, air show. Early flying machines drew huge crowds,

Below A dream of flight: a science
fiction novel of 1910 features the
futuristic 'Essex Ghost' on its cover.

Bottom Erich Mendelsohn's
prophetic airport sketch of 1914.

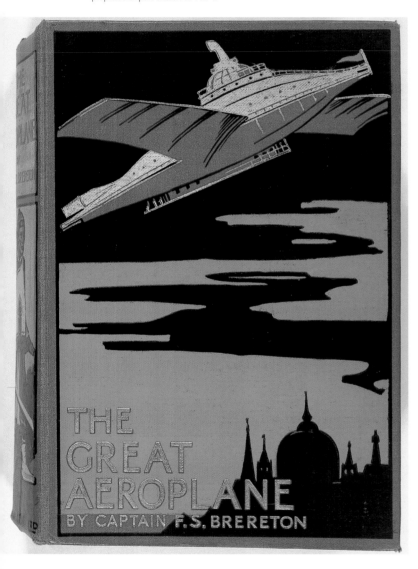

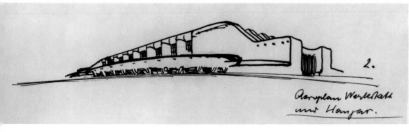

particularly if the show included a competitive element between the planes and
pilots – speed trials, distance and height trials and outright races being the norm.
The most important international example of the genre was the legendary Reims
Air Meet of 22–29 August 1909, based at the Betheny racetrack just outside
the famous French town.

What made this airshow significant was its timing. Only a month before, the
aviator Louis Blériot had made the first international flight, piloting his monoplane
50km (31 miles) across the English Channel on a dangerously windy day without
the benefit of a compass, to land on the clifftops near Dover Castle. So there
was huge public interest at the Reims show and – although there were hardly
two dozen planes in competition over the whole week – the crowds poured in,
with up to 500,000 people attending at a time. The organizers were expecting
them and had converted the circuit into a large aerodrome – the word by now
meaning an airfield rather than, as Langley had it, a flying machine. Along with
shops and a 600-seat restaurant looking out over the airfield, there were barbers
and beauty parlours, post and telegraph offices and – something that was to
become a feature of nearly all early airports – a large grandstand for spectators.
Circus acts kept people amused during the long periods when nothing seemed
to be happening. Indeed, the whole enterprise had a circus feel to it, with the
aviators taking the role of entertainers.

Photographs from the time show the already characteristic layout of an
L-shaped edge configuration of lightweight buildings, one section being for
spectators, the other for aviators and their oily occupations. Significantly,
passenger flights departed from there, with French pilot and plane-maker Henri
Farman (1874–1958) – who was to become a key figure in the development of
commercial aviation after World War One – winning a prize for ferrying two
spectators nearly 10km (6 miles). Taking notes that week was a future prime
minister of Britain, David Lloyd George, who remarked that planes were no
longer toys and dreams but established fact. As leader of his country during
World War One, Lloyd George was to approve a big expansion of military flying,
which was, in turn, to pave the way in Britain – as it did in Germany and France –
to post-war civil aviation. Former US President Theodore Roosevelt was also
present, though this had little effect back home. As we shall see, it is one of the
ironies of history that America – despite being the homeland of such pioneers as
the Wrights and Curtiss – was slow to adopt commercial flying, while Europe led
the way.

It has been pointed out by the architectural historian Wolfgang Voigt that all
the main air shows in France, Germany and Italy in 1908–9 adopted pretty much
the same layout, which was derived from land-based racing circuits. Indeed, if we
look at any horse-racing circuit today – with its grandstands and pavilions, its
ability to absorb large numbers of people over short periods and its effortless
manner of separating spectators from participants – we will see something like
those early airfields, an ancestry that continues to inform the design of airports
and their terminal buildings to this day. It seems unlikely, however, that anyone sat
down to design the ideal airfield. What they did do was sit down and plan an
event. To do this they resorted to the facilities and general layout familiar to them

Above A Grahame-White 'charabanc' at Hendon, 1913. It was able to carry four passengers.

Right Hendon was London's first serious airport, and it attracted large crowds at its pre-Great War airshows. Note in particular the hangars and control towers of the era.

from permanent racing circuits and also from fairgrounds, circuses and, to an extent, industrial expositions of the type that were hugely popular in the mid- to late 19th century. The Wright Brothers, pragmatic as ever, had meanwhile adopted their cow pasture at Huffman Prairie, not least because – although the cows had to be shooed to one side for take-offs and landings – they kept the turf short. Other early airfields used sheep for the same purpose.

The alternative pre-World War One model for an airport was provided by the DELAG company (Deutsche Luftshiffahrt Aktien Gesellschaft). This joint venture between von Zeppelin and the Hamburg-America Shipping Line was formed in 1909 – the year of Blériot, of the great air shows, of the Wrights' first military plane and thus of aviation miracles. DELAG was the world's first airline, and in 1910 its airship the *Deutschland* was the world's first commercial airliner. The company ran out-and-back trips from Friedrichshafen to such cities as Berlin, Düsseldorf and Hamburg, using four such rigid airships. By the outbreak of war they had carried at least 19,000 – some say nearly 34,000 – passengers.

DELAG took advantage of the fact that airships did not need land-hungry landing fields. Instead, they built interchange sheds within reach of the main railway stations in the cities visited. The sheds combined aspects of maintenance hangars and passenger terminals. The early DELAG operations tend to be dismissed by aviation purists on the grounds that these flights were essentially excursions rather than scheduled services, or that Zeppelins do not count, not having wings. But those are ludicrous quibbles. Large numbers of paying passengers were carried long distances in the air in very big, reliable flying machines at a surprisingly early date. Many of the people who looked up from their farms as the Zeppelins droned overhead would not even have seen a motor car. That same year, 1910, British newspapers were concerned that the nation would face a severe shortage of horses in the event of war. Five years later, Zeppelins – which, despite being vulnerable to attack, had a range and payload unmatched by any plane of the time – introduced the world to international aerial bombardment. Large planes were swiftly developed to take over this task.

Von Zeppelin's model of a relatively central civilian air terminal, not dissimilar to a railway terminus, did not endure, since even airships, being so large, had to move further out of town. However, one key aspect of his thinking survives to this day: the link between airports and rail systems. The link can be seen in the Futurist designs of Antonio Sant'Elia, whose machine-dominated imaginary metropolis, the Citta Nuova of 1913–14, foresees the layered, land-air transport interchanges of today. That much was prescient. What was not workable was the notion that air travel could be grafted on to existing city centres. It could not be – there was not enough space. Even so, that dream was to persist in some quarters up to the end of the 20th century.

It was one thing to append an aerodrome to an existing town or city – racetracks or military parade grounds suggested themselves there, with Blériot using the Champ de Manoeuvres parade ground at Issy-les-Moulineaux outside Paris – and in the United States, following the precedent of the Wrights' cow pasture, baseball grounds and polo fields were often used. It was another matter, however, to plan a complete new city, when more up-to-date architects would naturally tend to embrace the novel concept of the airport. So a significant international competition was held in 1912 for the proposed new Federal capital of Australia, later called Canberra. The key design – for our purposes, at least – is the one submitted by French architect Donat-Alfred Agache, which came third.

Agache (1875–1959) was a skilled urban planner who was in his prime at the time of the competition and fully aware of France's advanced developments in aviation. He drew perspectives of the proposed capital city from the point of view of an aviator flying both low and high. His drawing, entitled *Prospect view of Aerostatic Station: altitude 1200 feet,* sets out in beautifully drawn detail all the main elements of a modern airport as it was then imagined, with a variety of buildings surrounding a rectangular landing field, equipped for both airships and heavier-than-air planes, with the public (landside) buildings on one side of the field and the private (airside) buildings, such as maintenance hangars, on the other. Not that Agache got everything right. The flaw in his design was perhaps due to a Beaux Arts training that had inculcated in him a love of symmetry, a flaw that was to dog many realized airports down the years: he closed in his airfield neatly with buildings, so allowing no expansion space for future generations of large planes needing more space to land. This was particularly short-sighted, given that he placed his Aerostatic Station in green countryside on the outskirts, which would have allowed him all the expansion space he could need. Instead, he subconsciously designed a large, classical, urban piazza. Agache's proposed airfield looks relatively modern to our eyes because of its familiar oblong shape, which is the way the most recent airports and their parallel runways have tended to be configured. But this did not suit the flying machines of the day, which had to be able to take off into the wind, no matter which direction it came from.

The final significant model for an airport, as war intervened to hasten the whole process, was by Tony Garnier (1869–1948), the city architect of Lyons in France and a noted utopianist whose highly influential pet project, Une Cité Industrielle, first appeared in 1901–4. By 1917 he had revised his plan to include a well-conceived airport, for both planes and airships, with a trapezoidal landing field, 500m (½ mile) long, various buildings, including hangars and an aircraft factory – all kept well out of the way of planes, unlike Agache's earlier attempt – and a generally workaday feel to it: no big spectator stands. The war had removed some of the romance of flight, made it more commonplace. In a sensibly conceived urban plan, it clearly had a future.

Real airports were starting to appear. The first London airport was Hendon, way up on the northern rural fringes. It dated from 1909, when a local company built a plane and erected a shed in a field to accommodate it. By 1910 it was a fully operational airfield – where Blériot himself held flying lessons, just as the Wrights were doing at exactly the same time across the Atlantic at Huffman Prairie, which was developing an ad hoc collection of buildings in similar fashion. In 1911 Hendon was bought by the pilot, aircraft designer and manufacturer Claude Grahame-White (1879–1959), who renamed it the London Aerodrome and began an ambitious expansion. Later it became a Royal Air Force (RAF) airfield, and today it is the home of the RAF Museum. On waste ground to the south of the museum, the original Grahame-White office building with integral control tower, built in neo-Georgian manner in 1915–16 by architect Herbert Matthews, was still to be seen in a derelict state as this book was written.

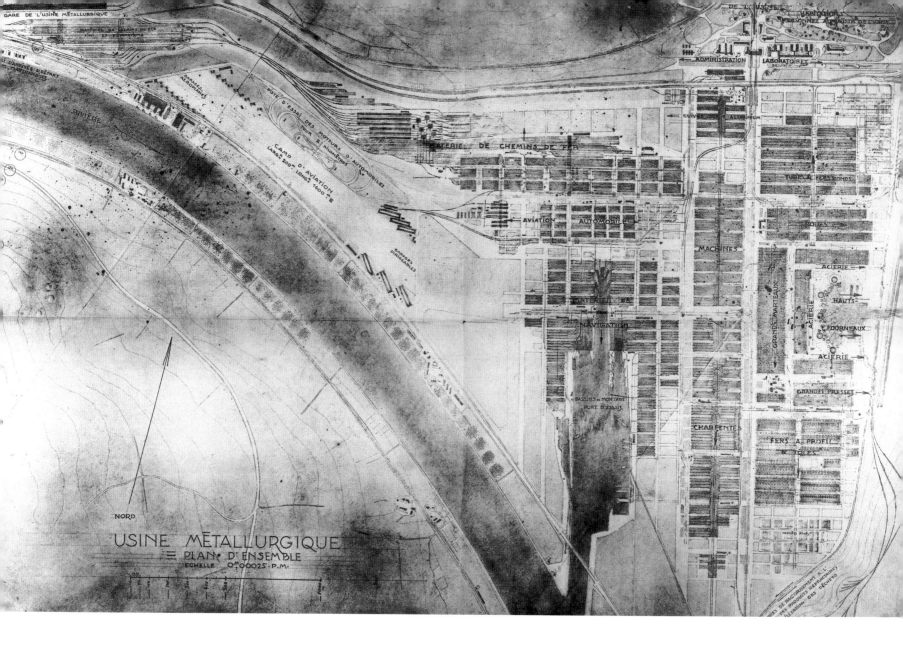

Above Tony Garnier's utopian Cité Industrielle project, begun in 1901, included a landing field by 1917. This is visible top left, and is attached to the factory zone.

Right Donat-Alfred Agache's plan for an 'aerostatic station' at Canberra, Australia, a competition entry, 1912.

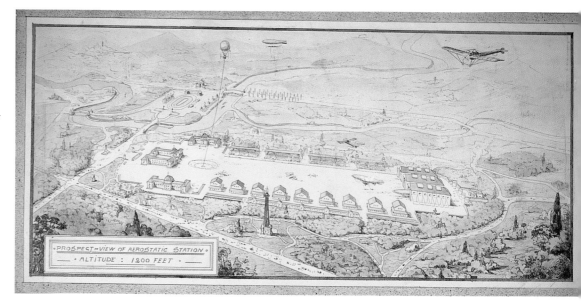

Above Duxford aerodrome, Cambridgeshire, in the early years of military aviation.

Below An early control tower at Hendon. The starter's box for air races included a booking office.

'Control tower' is perhaps pitching things a bit strong for something that was essentially a gazebo or belvedere: the whole ensemble was very like a cricket pavilion, complete with a lower balcony overlooking the airfield, which was noted for its pre-war air displays. Were a scoreboard to be erected in front of the stubby tower on top, the illusion would be complete.

In rather better shape than this evocative ruin is the former London Aerodrome Hotel of 1917, an exercise in half-timbered Tudorbethan style. Later an RAF officers' mess, it is now used as residences for university students. Hendon was a big operation for its day. Matthews also built a square of neo-Georgian cottages close by in 1917, called Aeroville, for the 300 employees of the London Aerodrome. Meanwhile, two surviving 1917–18 hangars of the Grahame-White aircraft factory demonstrate the shift from the 19th-century technology of timber lattice, Belfast trusses (also to be seen at the historic Duxford aerodrome in Cambridgeshire) to modern cross-braced, steel trusses. These hangars have now been restored as part of an expansion of the museum.

In September 1911 Grahame-White promoted a demonstration royal airmail service between London and Windsor, home of King George V. He held round-London air races attracting 500,000 spectators, so rivalling Reims. Several independent aircraft factories, including the famous Handley Page, set up in the neighbourhood. Dignitaries were ferried from Hendon to Paris for the Versailles Conference at the end of World War One. Given this successful start and the fact that the first British commercial airline, ATT, based its planes there, it is likely that, if things had been left to pursue their course, Hendon would have evolved into the main London airport. But the government intervened, and it was taken over by the RAF, which refused to return it to Grahame-White after the war and eventually bought him out.

Airfields had naturally proliferated during World War One, and some dating from that period, such as Duxford in Cambridgeshire (now an operational aviation museum), still possess some of the hangars and officers' clubrooms from that time. The planes had advanced in leaps and bounds, but not the airfields. In layout terms, little had changed since Huffman Prairie, although the military airfields had more buildings, and more permanent ones at that, since large numbers of people doing different tasks had to be housed. The preferred shape for airfields was circular, oval or (especially in the United States) square. They were turfed, often with the most commonly used parts overlaid with cinders or gravel and, where possible, slightly domed, to allow downhill runs into the wind in any direction. Paved runways were a relatively late invention and came into being because of the increasing weight of planes combined with the gradual reduction of their dependence on headwinds to get aloft.

Because the focus of the war had been in Europe, it was Europe, rather than the United States, that had the airfield infrastructure to move straight on to civilian aviation after the Armistice of 1918. The future began immediately after the cessation of hostilities. Heavier-than-air bombers, readily convertible to civilian use, were littering the airfields of Europe. In 1920 such a plane was the Goliath of the French aviation pioneer Henri Farman. It was the 747 of its day, able to transport 14 people in a comfortable cabin – already configured in the classic central-aisle manner – at 145kph (90mph), twice the speed of the

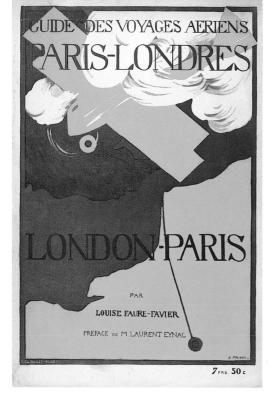

Above A passenger guide to the regular international commercial flight services between London and Paris, 1921. The plane represented is the Farman passenger aircraft.

Below Vaudeville takes to the air, in this illustration for a music sheet cover dating from 1918.

production Wright planes of a decade earlier. Farman and his rivals were soon able to develop such ex-military planes to carry more than 20 people at more than 160kph (100mph).

Commercial airlines were set up. Following DELAG's airships of 1910, a flying boat service ran passenger flights in south Florida briefly in 1914, using converted dock buildings. Regular passenger services resumed from 1919 in various places. There are conflicting claims as to who was first – there is some confusion as to the moment when military passenger-carrying services, sometimes operated by private entrepreneurs, went civilian – but it is generally accepted that Germany was first, with the airline DLR (Deutsche Luft Reederi) flying AEG biplanes between Berlin and Weimar from 22 February 1919. The first true international peacetime service by this reckoning was started by the British company Air Transport and Travel (ATT) between London Hounslow and Paris Le Bourget on 25 August 1919. It cost £21 to be one of only two passengers in a small but fast De Havilland biplane of the type that had been used for similar cross-Channel shuttle operations during the war.

Europe was not ahead in everything. The first regular United States airmail service departed from a polo field in Washington, D.C., on 15 May 1918. The US Postal Service was, in the years after World War One, pioneering in its use of planes. It developed a template for airfield design along its routes: five 'air stations' plus emergency landing places between New York and Chicago were in place by 1920. The Chicago hangar was paid for by local businesses and at $15,000 did not come cheap. A typical US Postal air station would be 610 x 610m (2,000 x 2,000ft), possess one hangar, a windsock and a telephone line, have a cinder or gravel surface over earth and feature a tall location marker incorporating a light beacon rated at 500,000 candlepower. To this example, we may add all the ad hoc municipal airfields springing up on patches of land near towns and cities across the United States, and the more formalized airfields laid out by US plane manufacturers such as Curtiss. The big difference, however, was this: in America, everything was left to the private sector. Not until the late 1920s was there a government-led push to plan and encourage airports. In contrast, the European airports were state sponsored from the start. Although America was consequently late to adopt civil aviation wholeheartedly, this did have one advantage: it meant that when it did, in the 1930s, it was able to skip a generation and build a modern generation of airports with runways.

London, Paris and Berlin were the European node points where the earliest international airports developed. The picture is distinct in Paris and Berlin, where the former military grounds of Le Bourget and Tempelhof, both within a few miles of their respective city centres, were adopted early and developed consistently. London, a more diffuse city than its Continental rivals, took some time to settle on a main airport site, juggling its airfields in the north (Hendon), south (Croydon) and west (Hounslow), all at a greater distance from the centre than its French and German counterparts. London's parade grounds were too small, because British armies were by long tradition kept well dispersed and away from the capital, apart from a relatively token security presence. The only serviceable open space near the centre of London happened to consist of interlinked royal parks arranged around palaces, and even in the first flush of aviation enthusiasm,

Above A Farman Goliath of the type
beloved by Le Corbusier.

Above A public demonstration in Hendon's Edwardian heyday, 1911.

Below As early as 1909, the advertising potential of dirigibles was being exploited. The inset portrait shows aviator Comte Henry de La Vaulx.

Opposite *Goodbye Kiss*: an illustration from the 1920s shows the elite way to travel.

e dirigeable « LE PETIT JOURNAL » atterrissant sur la pelouse de Bagatelle

nobody considered using them for a moment, any more than Republican New York gave over Central Park. Even in the swashbuckling mid-19th century, when the railways cut brutal swathes through outer London, they were not allowed to trespass on the historic centre.

Hounslow Heath had been an airfield in 1910. It had become a wartime centre but was relinquished by the RAF in May 1919 and was renamed the London Terminal Aerodrome in clear rivalry with Hendon. Winning the race to be the first declared British 'customs airport', it was licensed to handle international traffic and was hence the place that ATT was obliged to embark and disembark its passengers. Services began in August 1919, but its reign was short, for in March 1920 the government had completed its airfield shuffling exercise and opened its preferred airport at Croydon, some distance to the south of London. The west would eventually triumph, however, since the area continued to house aircraft maker Fairey, who bought adjacent land near the village of Heathrow and built the Great West Aerodrome. This subsequently became a bomber base in World War Two and, after the war, London's main civilian airport, still expanding today.

All that was for the future. All those former fields, sports grounds, parade grounds and racetracks, with their interesting but ramshackle collections of sheds, tents and hangars, first had to develop into something else. Until the start of the 1920s enough 'permanent' airfield buildings and structures had obviously been built to serve only flying machines and their pilots and mechanics, plus other military personnel. Essentially, they were large workshops and garages with some administrative offices, a clubhouse or mess, and sometimes sleeping accommodation. Hangars were needed not just for maintenance, but also to store planes that could not be left out in bad weather – which meant they had to be stored for several months each winter, when flying did not take place. Because regular commercial passenger services were only just beginning, there had been little need previously to consider those people who were not intimately acquainted with the workings of a Gnome rotary engine or with the operation of a joystick.

These other people were passengers, who had to be accommodated in ways that were different from those provided for the excited land-based, day-tripping spectators of the pre-war air shows; or the early enthusiasts for air travel who were prepared to rough it. They were delicate live cargo to be carried, they were wealthy, powerful and articulate, and they would not be pleased if they got oil on their cashmere coats or their fine leather suitcases. A new kind of building had to be devised to cope with these non-operational, demanding and slightly frightening humans, buildings that would both cater for them and flatter them. The result that followed was to be some of the most evocative architecture of the inter-war years.

In Europe, where the principles of aviation were well established, the modern airport swiftly emerged in the inter-war years, as countries established a network of international and internal routes. For a while the United States was on the back foot. It lacked the military aviation infrastructure of Europe, and anyway regarded rail and road as the best means of transporting people. It is arguable that Henry Ford's development of the mass-produced car initially set back the cause of US aviation. Cars became cheap, plentiful and reliable, putting consumers fully in control and leading to the building of the best highways in the world. What need was there for expensive, unreliable flights where passengers were at the mercy of others and their cherished freedoms much curtailed?

Ford (1863–1947) later entered the aviation industry and played catch-up. The amazingly successful Model T had been introduced in 1909, and by the mid-1920s it was nearing the end of its long production run. By now the car industry was packed with rivals, and Ford was struggling to repeat his first success. The air industry, however, was comparatively open, and Ford tackled the new

Chapter Two A New Building Type

challenge in some style, most famously with the advanced and popular all-metal Tri-Motor airliner, known as the Tin Goose. Charles Lindbergh was his chief test pilot. In 1925–6 the Ford Dearborn airport in Michigan was the first to be designed and built with permanent concrete runways, and although it was a company base, it served as the main airport for the Detroit area for a number of years and was complete with restaurant, hotel and (naturally) limousine service to downtown Detroit.

The buildings of Ford Dearborn airport were designed by the great industrial architect Albert Kahn (1869–1942), the designer of Ford's factories. Ford employed Kahn again to build a companion airport at Lansing, near Chicago, and this had a 'hangar-depot', a feature common to inter-war American airports, where planes and passengers and staff mingled in one big building, just as in the earliest days of aviation. Such private airports were the pattern in the 1920s, with the Curtiss-Wright company building a chain of 12 by 1930. It made sense: without airports to serve them, nobody would buy the planes. America was in the curious position of being technologically advanced as far as the vehicles were concerned but backward when it came to providing the buildings to serve them.

Between 1926 and 1933 a total of 199 Tri-Motors were built, and the plane was as instrumental in bringing forward the fledgling US airline industry as Ford Dearborn was in anticipating future airports. Ford could have gone on to be as big as Boeing, rather as Britain's Rolls-Royce was to become a world force in aero-engines. Yet interestingly, Henry Ford – whose company was formed in 1903, the year of the Wrights' first flight, who was friendly with the brothers and who at first used Wright Whirlwind engines in the Tri-Motor – lost interest in commercial flight after the crash in testing of a single-seater plane that he envisaged as the airborne equivalent of the Model T car.

There was still a desire for a personal, unregulated form of flying, which would require nothing like an airline industry arranged like railways or shipping lines, with big buildings to herd passengers through. Instead, there would be a plane in every garage. But with the collapse of that dream, Ford's interest in, and influence over, civil aviation was effectively at an end, although Kahn later designed Ford's World War Two bomber factory at Willow Run, Detroit. Ford

Above The first Tempelhof terminal,
in Berlin, by Paul and Klaus Engler,
1926–9, was an extrudable piece of
Modernist architecture.

Opposite A Ford Tri-Motor at
Dearborn, in front of buildings by
Albert Kahn. Ford's flirtation with flight
was to be short-lived.

Previous Gatwick airport terminal in
the 1930s, designed by Hoar, Marlow
and Lovett.

Dearborn is these days predominantly a car proving ground, although Lansing is
still operational as a regional airport. Before all this, however, in the early 1920s,
America's geographical isolation from World War One meant that it did not share
a particularly European feeling: that international flight could in some way help to
heal the divisions between previously warring nations and could even help to melt
borders. It was a hope that had preceded the war. In 1935 the architect Le
Corbusier recalled an incident of 1909 when his colleague, Auguste Perret, burst
in, brandishing a newspaper and exclaiming: 'Blériot has crossed the Channel!
Wars are finished: no more wars are possible! There are no longer any frontiers!'

Despite the carnage of World War One, this desire was not extinguished. In
retrospect it seems an absurdly optimistic notion, but every new communications
technology, from the wireless to the Internet, tends to engender similar hopes.
The idea is always the same: that if there is freer communication between the
people of different nations and cultures they will understand each other better,
and this understanding will reduce the risk of conflict. The history of Europe
might seem directly to contradict this view, but there it was: aviators were seen
as heroes capable of extraordinary achievements. The land war in 1914–18 had
been horrific, but although Zeppelins had briefly bombed British cities and the
young aviators had a life expectancy measured in hours rather than days, planes
had yet to be associated with mass slaughter. Despite the prophetic warning
uttered by H.G. Wells in his science-fiction novel *The War in the Air* (1908),
flight was to retain much of that air of innocence up to the Spanish Civil War
(1936–9), when it proved the deadliest of activities. This may be why airports of
the inter-war years have a more joyous spirit than those post-World War Two.

All pictures Flying from Croydon in
the 1930s: Imperial Airways planes
were slow but very reliable. The
clothes and cars of the travellers
reveal their wealth in this illustration
from 1926 (above) and early
photographs from the 1930s.

For a variety of reasons, therefore, the main development of the airport passed
from America to Europe, and this resulted in some frustration among forward-
looking Americans who felt that the United States was losing out economically
as a result. In the summer of 1928 Lieutenant Colonel Stedman S. Hanks of the
United States Air Corps Reserve toured the bustling airports of Europe and
published his findings in New York the following year. 'As yet there are very few
American airports that handle international traffic … it is in operating
international air services that Europe has the most marked advantages over
America,' wrote Hanks. His mission in Europe was simply 'for the purpose of
learning in what ways their greater experience in international air traffic could
serve as a useful guide for airport construction and management in this country
… Perhaps it will be helpful also in making Americans more air-minded.'

Hanks cannot keep the admiration out of his narrative, and he retains all the
enthusiasm of Perret from 20 years previously when Blériot had flown the
English Channel. 'It is hard to believe that ten years ago, no foundations had
been started, no concrete had been laid, and no grass had been grown on any
so-called commercial airport of today. In most cases there was only a large area
of gravel or underbrush in most of the present fields,' he wrote, somehow
forgetting the vital contribution of military infrastructure. 'Today the map of
Europe is peppered with active airports. They are busy the whole day and even at
night: such is progress, which makes us forget quarrels, wipes out frontiers, and
binds nations together.'

He goes on to quote a London newspaper of 20 September 1928, which
reported that Germany had 160 airliners, flying more than 64,3000km (40,000
miles) each day and carrying nearly 20,000 passengers a month. In 1928 at
Berlin's Tempelhof airport alone, Hanks adds, 41,214 passengers arrived or
departed, together with 285 tonnes (280 tons) of baggage and 275 tonnes
(270 tons) of freight.

Hanks regarded Berlin's Tempelhof and London's Croydon as model airports,
which America should emulate. Croydon, he said, was 'one of the best-equipped
and operated air terminals in the world'. He has some praise for a few American
examples of the period – Buffalo, New York, dating from 1925–8, with its three
cinder runways and steel-framed hangars, Chicago, with its passenger waiting
room, post office and shops, and Oakland, California, with a 150-seat restaurant
– but he was far more enamoured of the more sophisticated European model.

His report was essentially accurate. For all the pioneering work of the Wrights,
Curtiss, the US Postal Service and, later, Ford and Lindbergh, America lagged
about a decade behind Europe in the development of commercial passenger
aviation. London's Hounslow had processed passengers through a wartime
hangar, and Croydon built a grand classical terminal, which opened in 1928.
There, in 1924, several independent airlines had already coalesced into Imperial
Airways, the forerunner of today's British Airways. Britain was already on to its
second generation of commercial airport while America was still struggling to get
the first generation established.

By the mid-1920s, however, things were starting to take shape in the United
States. Chicago's first airport, later renamed Midway, opened in 1927, and in
1931 a modern terminal building with some Art Deco internal details was added

Above Where's the terminal? The first Paris Le Bourget in the 1920s featured small buildings around a civic square instead.

Left The first integrated modern airport terminal, Königsberg in East Prussia, was designed by Hans Hopp in 1922.

by city architect Paul Gerhardt. As Lieutenant Bert Shoemaker, supervisor of the city's first airfield in 1922, said: 'Chicago is destined to be the air center of the world.' The sentiment was repeated in 1961 by the city's commissioner of aviation, William E. Downes, who said: 'Once the crossroads of America, Chicago is now the crossroads of the world.' This did not come about immediately. Delays were to beset plans to build Chicago a new, larger airport, and the two additional facilities at lakeside Meigs Field (designed for both land planes and flying boats) and inland O'Hare were not developed until well after World War Two. Midway was a portent, but it was not yet in the European league.

Paris Le Bourget and Berlin Tempelhof have similar, if simpler, stories than the London airports described in Chapter 1. At Le Bourget, less than 13km (8 miles) from the centre of Paris, commercial concerns took over ex-military hangars and buildings on the eastern edge of the airfield. These began to be replaced with new, classical buildings in the early 1920s, with the functions divided among several such buildings, which were arranged around a formal garden. This was not, however, to be the blueprint for the modern airport terminal. Wolfgang Voigt cites the airport of Königsberg (formerly the capital of East Prussia, now Kaliningrad in Russia) as the first true terminal and dates it to 1922, when its architect, Hans Hopp, placed all its passenger and administrative functions in a single, tiered building in one corner of a rectangular airfield, with big hangars to either side. It was called an air station. The airport was built to help relieve the political isolation of East Prussia, left adrift from the rest of Germany by the Treaty of Versailles in 1919.

Königsberg might be regarded as a dry run for the big one, Tempelhof in Berlin, which had been a venue for air shows and demonstrations before World War One. Tempelhof is perhaps the single most important airport in the history of aviation, and its lessons are still being learned. Although London and Paris got going sooner – Tempelhof did not open for commercial aviation until 1923 – Weimar Germany took to commercial aviation with greater gusto than any other nation in the world. Both the first Modernist Tempelhof terminal, built by Paul and Klaus Engler in 1926–9, and the second, neoclassical one, built by Ernst Sagebiel in the late 1930s, were examples to the world. Following the normal pattern of the time, the Englers built hangars for the planes first, then a central radio station/control tower, then finally the passenger building, which was arranged as a two-storey, strip building (plus central attic part-storey) and set behind the tower. It had the obligatory restaurant roof terrace. The linear, strip-windowed building was handled with considerable aplomb, with vertical emphasis being given by two tall steel radio masts standing like spires in front.

As designers of airports were to discover time after time, there are two kinds of expansion to consider. One is the expansion of the terminal to handle increased passenger numbers. The Englers allowed for this, and their building was designed to extend at each end. Before too long, however, the second problem arose: the need to expand the landing field to cope with larger numbers of bigger, faster, heavier planes. The Englers, or their clients, had not considered this, despite the laudable precedent of Königsberg, where the buildings were placed in one corner. At Tempelhof the terminal was in the wrong place, out towards the middle, and when Sagebiel came to design its replacement, he duly

Below Already hemmed in by development in the 1930s, Chicago's Midway shows a complex interlocking runway layout dictated by the need to take off into the wind.

pulled the enormous building complex right back to the perimeter, giving it a real urban presence that befitted a terminal so very close to the city centre. With its traditional landside architecture, the second, Nazi-era Tempelhof looks and feels more like a grand railway terminus than an airport.

One of the things that most captivated Hanks about European airports was their restaurants. He devoted a section of his book to the design of the ideal airport eaterie, which – though he does not say so – sounds very like an amalgam of Croydon, Tempelhof and Le Bourget: 'Comfortable reception rooms artistically furnished, a roof-garden commanding a wide view over the whole aviation field, and spacious terraces with chairs and tables in the lawns invite the visitor to stay. The catering is in the hands of a well-known railway Pullman car service or hotel restaurant company.'

At this same Tempelhof at the start of the 21st century people could sit in a restaurant in a central terminal building, overlooking planes arriving and departing on the apron below, and with just that 'wide view over the whole aviation field' that Hanks described. Of course, this is a feature of many airports today – though the clarity tends to be lost as the organism grows – but at Tempelhof the circumstances were different from the norm. The view was overshadowed by a large external roof, supported on a tough, column-free latticework, cantilevered from great wings of buildings curving round to a vanishing point on either side. One might assume that these subsidiary buildings are the departure gates – the classic wingspread plan of the modern airport – but no. The design of this airport dates from the mid-1930s.

Just as the railway terminus was the most evocative building type of the 19th century, the air terminal became the equivalent in the 20th century. Of all of these, Tempelhof became the most enduring exemplar. Its great time was in 1948–9, the period of the Berlin Airlift, when planes arrived and departed every few seconds to bring supplies to the besieged Berliners. Such a flow of planes made an almost solid aerial connection – the German word for that extraordinary event, *luftbrücke*, airbridge, describes it almost exactly. It was a road across the sky. The density of air traffic in those years more than anticipated today's crowded skies, and the airport coped superbly. But this Tempelhof did not spring from nowhere. It drew on an earlier influence.

Sagebiel was inspired by his former master, Erich Mendelsohn (1887–1953), who had been forced into exile by the Nazi regime. It can be argued that Tempelhof is the airport that Mendelsohn never built, in circumstances he could never have envisaged when, at the age of 27 – just before his military service in World War One – he designed the giant airport (see page 36), which was as prescient as the glamorous contemporary designs of the Futurists were flawed.

Mendelsohn had envisaged a large, reinforced-concrete building, some 400–460m (1,300–1,500ft) long. He had imagined a curving plan, with a tall central hall to handle six airships and low hangars for aeroplanes and workshops to either side. Several early airport designs featured large, centrally placed airship hangars, and it is interesting to note that when airship travel all but ceased after the disasters of the 1930s, the architectural form of the large central space could be commandeered for use as the passenger terminal. This is how Sagebiel adapted his former master's speculative aerodrome design at Tempelhof.

Above Hugh Casson's 1947 Modernist sketch of the interior of the terminal at Glasgow airport.

Above The second Tempelhof by Ernst Sagebiel was intended as the hub of German air power. Seen here post-war, it was largely built from 1935 to 1939.

Right This aerial view of the second Tempelhof, illustrated on a 1940–1 calender, shows the vast extent of the complex. It was second in size only to the Pentagon in Washington.

DEZEMBER/JANUAR

28	29	30	31	1	2	3
SONNTAG	MONTAG	DIENSTAG	MITTWOCH	DONNERST.	FREITAG	SONNABEND
				NEUJAHR		

Above The frame of the Akron airdock under construction.

Above Left Akron hangar 2. Such buildings rotated into the wind.

Left A colossal rotating structure: the airdock for the US airship Akron, in 1929. Vertical sliding doors gave way to clamshell openings.

Above This 1936 poster is an advertisement for the German Zeppelin Shipping Company. It reads 'Crossing the ocean in two days'. Transatlantic travel carried the flag for Nazi Germany's regime.

Mendelsohn had had a clear idea of the modern, all-embracing airport terminal building. He anticipated what would develop in the inter-war years at London's Croydon, at Paris's Le Bourget, at New York's La Guardia, at Atlanta, Georgia, and finally at Sagebiel's Tempelhof, which was designed to last until the year 2000, and, somewhat surprisingly, did. Its fate – latterly as a lightly used commuter-plane hub – was sealed with the fall of the Berlin Wall in 1989 and subsequent reunification of Germany. Along with Berlin's other main airport, Tegel, it is destined to be replaced by the single new airport of Berlin-Brandenburg. This will be on the site of the former East Berlin airport of Schönefeld, which was due to close in 2004. However, Tempelhof succeeded in being the only major airport in the world to have remained virtually unchanged for more than 60 years – a period in which the nature of air travel changed completely. It was a part of history that went on living, like a coelacanth.

Tempelhof survived so long for three main reasons. First, air travel in and out of West Berlin was necessarily limited during the Cold War when it was an isolated pocket of West Germany surrounded by the East – strangely recalling that prototype modern airport terminal at Königsberg in isolated East Prussia, as long ago as 1922. Second, the newer Berlin post-war airport with longer runways, Tegel, eventually relieved pressure on the old place, leaving it as a centre for smaller planes on mainly internal routes. But crucially, Sagebiel designed Tempelhof with a massive redundancy of space. It anticipated the growth of air travel to an extraordinary extent, simply by being greatly oversized to start with.

It had been first conceived in 1933, shortly after Hitler came to power and Mendelsohn quit Germany, as a grandiose expression of national pride. In this it was unlike the Englers' earlier, 1925–9 terminal at Tempelhof, which had been modestly designed on what became the classic pattern of the separately expressed central control tower with gently curving wings for accommodation to either side. Its life was effectively over after less than a decade – although World War Two was to extend its life since Sagebiel's replacement terminal, though largely complete, was not brought into use until the war was over. Near completion, it was greatly admired by another American commentator, a successor to Hanks, John Walter Wood. In a book of 1940, written after just such a fact-finding sweep round Europe's airports as Hanks had undertaken a decade before, Wood compared 40 US and European examples, and noted that Orville Wright had made several demonstration flights at Tempelhof as early as 1909, when it was still a parade ground. Of Sagebiel's Tempelhof, with its landing area now tripled to 540 hectares (1,333 acres) from that of the Englers' earlier plan, he remarked: 'It has been said that the new airport has been planned on too vast a scale for practical use. Exactly the same criticism was made of the 1925 terminal, and that view was proved groundless, as is now so apparent.'

Wood did feel that Sagebiel's huge, cantilevered, plane-protecting roof was 'unnecessary and wasteful' and that it failed as a system properly to segregate arriving and departing passengers. Whether or not Wood was aware of US and British experiments with retractable covered ways – the forerunners of today's airbridges – from terminal to planes (see page 58), is not clear. But he suggested: 'A covered passenger platform would accomplish the same purpose at less expense and without limiting the dimensions of planes.'

Above and below Gatwick airport's circular 'beehive' terminal by Hoar, Marlow and Lovett is shown in an early model (below) and a BA advertisement in a Covent Garden opera programme from 1936 (above).

Thanks to Tempelhof's curious history – which may be traced from Mendelsohn to the beginnings of airport design, from its even earlier connection with Orville Wright to its sullying association with the Nazis, cleansed by its association with the Airlift, and now preserved as if in aspic by its unusual size and relative isolation – we see how airports can be as much political as planning, design and architectural statements. A big airport is a concern of the state. An airport is generally always being rebuilt precisely because people can hardly ever bring themselves to allow enough for future expansion. A nation is therefore always having to plan future airports, always struggling to handle ever-increasing capacity. And of course, an airport is a gateway. Tempelhof was virtually the last to be sited so close to a city centre, where its civic presence is as urbanistically strong as the Brandenburg Gate. But the most important planning decision made in both the Englers' terminal and its Sagebiel successor was to keep to a minimum the distance walked by a passenger between the landside set-down outside and the planes waiting airside.

Although Sagebiel was not as successful in achieving transparency, in many respects his Tempelhof is Mendelsohn's Expressionist 1914 aerodrome design in disguise. The tall central hall is there, although for people rather than airships. The curving wings, with their configuration of hangars and workshops, are there. The proportions are slightly different, and the elevational style is wholly different, but Sagebiel had learned well from his old master. Do not be fooled by the surface appearance: this is a very modern, efficient building, just as the Gothic fantasy of Sir George Gilbert Scott's Midland Hotel at St Pancras Station in London (1868–74) conceals an ideal plan for what was then a new building type, the rail terminus.

In the early years of air travel the terminal buildings played host to spectators as much as travellers. People went there for a day out. Terminals such as the one that was built in Dublin in 1937–41 by Desmond Fitzgerald and the Office of Public Works (see Chapter 4) were designed accordingly, with cantilevered viewing platforms at either end of the curving accommodation wing. The Englers' first Tempelhof could seat 3,000 on top, and in 1929 it received 750,000 visitors. Sagebiel had intended to continue this tradition on a predictably grand scale, envisaging a raised stand for 65,000 spectators on his roof – no doubt he had air shows and military rallies in mind. He built 14 staircases to the roof – they are still visible – to serve this one-sided stadium before the war stopped work.

In the 1930s another prototype of the post-war terminal was being tested in Britain. In 1930 an extendible access corridor to aircraft had been tried at Boeing's United airport at Burbank, California. It was a fairly simple telescoping canopy rather than a tube. In 1936 Gatwick airport took the idea much further. Then called London South, the airport, which was some 40km (25 miles) from the capital, was given an express rail link – the first in Europe. The London–Paris trip, which included a first-class rail ticket from London's Victoria Station, cost £4 5s (£4.25) and took two and a half hours. The service began on Sunday, 17 May 1936. Architects Hoar, Marlow and Lovett designed a circular terminal, accessed directly by subway from the rail station. Six 'gates' led to radiating, lightweight, rigid, rectangular telescopic tubes complete with windows, each in three sections and sliding on rails, which delivered the passengers under shelter to their aircraft.

Above and right Dublin airport in the 1930s, designed by Desmond Fitzgerald and the Office of Public Works. The interior shows it in its glory during the 1950s.

Below The ground floor plan of the Dublin terminal shows how it curves away from the airfield rather than embracing it.

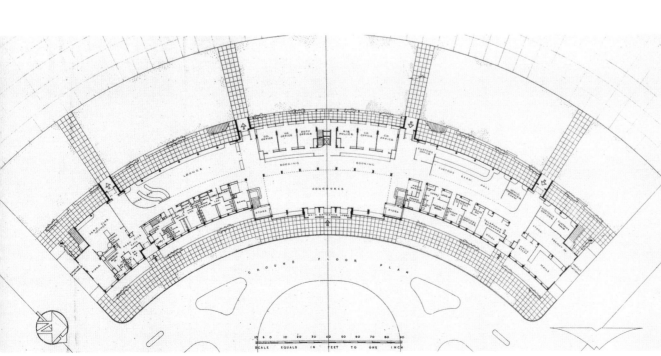

The building, known as the Beehive, survives today as airline offices, although the telescopic tunnels have gone. This type of structure, further developed in the post-war years, was in essence the model taken for the first phase of Paris Charles de Gaulle at Roissy in the late 1960s and thence all circular terminals and satellites. Croydon, dating from the 1920s, could not compete with this progressive design, but it was advanced in ways perhaps belied by its rather ponderous classical architecture by Air Ministry architects. Hanks approved of one innovation. Although it still had a predominantly turfed, runway-free 'all-way field' from which planes could take off and land in any direction, it was equipped with a pattern of landing lights that were changed from the control tower according to wind direction.

At Le Bourget, meanwhile, it was necessary to correct the architectural false start of the early 1920s. With its discrete buildings around an open space rather than an all-purpose terminal, Le Bourget was stuck in a timewarp. The 1922 reinforced-concrete hangars by architect Henri Lossier (still to be seen today) were easily the most interesting buildings from that period. Ancillary buildings in general from this time remain fascinating because of the engineering prowess they exhibit: Eugene Freyssinet's reinforced-concrete airship hangars (1917) at Paris Orly, France; the huge airdocks (1917–27) at Cardington, Bedfordshire, UK, for airships such as the R100 and R101; the wind tunnels at the Royal Aircraft Establishment at Farnborough, Hampshire, UK, now a private airport and business park; Pier Luigi Nervi's latticework-construction hangar (1935) at the Orvieto air force base in Italy. Airport designers got the large, clear-span spaces in hangars sorted out long before they got to grips with the passenger terminals. Architect Georges Labro was the man to put Le Bourget right, rebuilding it to follow the now proven single-terminal pattern of Tempelhof and Croydon.

Clearly with an eye on Sagebiel's still-emerging design in Berlin, Labro designed a long, repeated modular building entered on axis through a wider and taller central bay with an engaged square tower on the landside and a curvilinear projecting wing topped with a control tower on the airside. Built in 1936–7, this second Le Bourget terminal is an exact diagram of the modern airport: arrival and car parking, people-processing a short distance through a central zone, then dispersal to the aircraft drawn up on the apron just outside. Although it was done in horizontal moderne style, complete with metal-framed strip windows, rather than the starchier stripped-classical elevations of Sagebiel's Tempelhof with its vertical emphasis, in one way at least Le Bourget was still not as advanced as its Berlin rival. There was still no means of getting from terminal to plane under cover. But as an expression of Modernist intent, it was and is remarkable. Its reinforced-concrete construction and almost blindingly white limestone façades, together with its internal top-lighting through glass pavement lenses and stately interiors, make it the most single-minded, least compromised airport terminal of its generation. Now the French air and space museum, with its airfield the site of the biennial Paris air show, Labro's terminal, with its cool, confident architecture, still encapsulates much of the spirit of the age.

Architecture buffs do not regard dull Croydon, for all its strategic and technical importance, as being a worthy member of this inter-war European troika. The Air Ministry architects produced a solid but uninspired building, complete with an

Opposite Q121 wind tunnel at Royal Aircraft Establishment, Farnborough, England, 1935. It was used to test full-size planes and has now been preserved as an historic artefact.

Above Freyssinet's hangars at Paris
Orly, 1917, dwarf the neoclassical
buildings in the foreground.

Below Cardington airship docks,
England, 1917–27, still exist today as
research buildings.

Opposite Pier Luigi Nervi's open-
sided hangar at Orvieto, Italy, in 1935, is
a virtuoso gridshell construction.

Above A modern image, but still no cover from terminal to plane at the second Le Bourget, illustrated here in 1938.

Below Speke airport, Liverpool, was an exercise in late Art Deco. This photograph was taken in 1947.

adjacent hotel, but if it were not for the large, square control tower, it could have been a lesser 19th-century railway station. Instead, aficionados of the pioneering terminals point to Speke in Liverpool (1937–8) as the British answer to the continental airport architecture of the time. Speke was built at the same time as Sagebiel's Tempelhof and Le Bourget, so it may be directly compared with them. Where the Englers' Tempelhof was Modern, Sagebiel's was neoclassical and Labro's Le Bourget was moderne, Speke was and is late Art Deco. This style was not so uncommon in some of the American airports that were starting to emerge at this time, but in Europe, where chaster styles prevailed, it is a glorious exception. Its unexpected grandeur for a provincial airport is due to the fact that Liverpool, as Britain's premier Atlantic port and historic point of departure for both Ireland and America, was a prosperous city that had no intention of missing out on the new form of transport and intended to make its mark.

A delegation from Liverpool studied the airports of Amsterdam, Berlin and Hamburg and was most impressed by the latter. Hamburg, like Liverpool a major port, had put its airport at Fuhlsbüttel out to an architectural competition, which was won by Friedrich Dryssen and Peter Averhoff. Built in 1928, Fuhlsbüttel was regarded by commentators of the day as certainly the equal of, possibly the superior to, the Englers' Tempelhof. It was of brick, it curved, it had viewing terraces and an engaged central control tower, and it was centrally placed between two large hangars. Cleanly modern, there was not a touch of Art Deco about it. Indeed, with its tiers of spectators and large picture windows, it looked

This page The second Le Bourget,
by Georges Labro in 1936–7, put right
the mistakes of the first, and
pioneered the linear terminal.

more like an upmarket racecourse grandstand than anything. All these cues were picked up for Speke, which was a larger, later and altogether brassier affair.

The task of designing Speke – a levelled patch of land on the Mersey estuary a few miles south of Liverpool, originally intended as a seaplane terminus – fell to architect Edward Bloomfield, who had trained in Charles Rennie Mackintosh's Art Nouveau Glasgow School of Art and who worked in Liverpool's architects' department under the man whose name appears on the plans, chief city architect Albert D. Jenkins. The steel-framed, brick-clad building with its tall, central, octagonal control tower and flanking pair of large hangars is a superb set-piece even today, when the terminal building has been converted into a hotel (and extended rearwards in pastiche Art Deco style), while the larger of the two hangars with its Art Deco clerestory is today a fitness centre. Bloomfield disengaged his control tower and set it proud, wrapping the terminal around behind it and stepping it down from centre to ends. The plan of Fuhlsbüttel lurks within a considerably more ornate carapace. By then this plan, with its ineluctable logic, was accepted as the norm.

Speke also learned from its Hamburg precedent in the way it segregated the functions of the terminal, keeping spectators and restaurant diners away from passengers, and setting up the key ingredient of all terminals today: the system whereby passengers leave their luggage at a check-in desk and proceed upstairs (usually) to departures. The era of everyone milling around together was already over by 1928, and flying, in Weimar Germany at least, was a serious and professional business. No wonder the burghers of Liverpool looked there rather than to home-grown precedents.

Behind these European leaders others were coming up fast. Dirk Roosenburg's terminal at Amsterdam's Schipol (1929), in the Dutch rationalist manner, took its cue from the German models but was also clearly influenced by Willem Dudok's contemporary Hilversum Town Hall. Schipol was busy even then and housed what is today the longest surviving of all the world's airlines, KLM, which dates from 1919. KLM thus predates the airport itself, which started in 1920 on a polder (reclaimed land) some 4m (13ft) below sea level. Even so, this agreeable little asymmetrical, L-shaped pavilion with attached semicircular tower – rather like the railway signal boxes of the time – gave little clue as to how enormous and vital Schipol was to become in European aviation. Largely destroyed by bombing in 1940, it was rebuilt after the war.

Every country brought its own architectural heritage to the building of the airport. In America there was at first no consensus as to the appropriate style. Kansas's Fairfax airport (1929) by Charles A. Smith was Art Deco; Washington airport (1930) by Holden, Scott and Hutchinson was moderne; the first St Louis airport and the first (1931) New York airport terminal at Floyd Bennett Field were neocolonial; Albuquerque (1936–9) by Ernest H. Blumenthal was in the adobe manner; and a number of west coast airports, including most notably San Francisco (1937) by H.G. Chipier, were in Spanish-pueblo style; Chicago as we have seen was International Modern, while Miami and New York's later La Guardia, both by Delano and Aldrich, concocted a style of moderne going on Art Deco, despite the fact that William Adams Delano, the man responsible, was in the twilight of a career that had until that point been one of accomplished

Below Hamburg Fuhlsbüttel, 1928, was taken as the model for the later Speke airport.

Opposite Speke was the main destination for flights from Ireland in the 1930s and 1940s.

Above Albuquerque, New Mexico, US, by Ernest H. Blumenthal, adopted the adobe style both inside and out.

Right Like a 1930s railway signal box: Roosenburg's Schipol control tower, Amsterdam.

Below Dirk Roosenburg's 1929 Schipol terminal. The open-air cafes show how much air travel was still a spectator sport.

Right Czech functionalism at Prague,
1933–7, by Adolf Bens.

Below The interior of Roosenburg's
Schipol airport, 1929.

neoclassical mansions and clubhouses. South America showed a similar diversity
but with perhaps a greater leaning towards the Modern. In Europe, after the
Edwardian neoclassical style quickly played itself out, the preferred style was
Modernism in all its variants – though for a colonial airport such as Al Basra in
Iraq (1937–8) British architects Wilson and Mason were allowed to build what
looked like a grand imperial palace for Imperial Airways.

The German/Dutch brick aesthetic differed markedly from hard-edged white
French Modernism, though not necessarily the Spanish. The Barajas airport
terminal in Madrid (1929–31) by Luis Gutierrez Soto was paradoxically Dutch
through and through. Different also was the advanced Czech functionalism seen
in Prague's terminal (1933–7) by Adolf Bens, the related circular Budaors airport
in Budapest (1937) by Virgil Borbiro and Lasalo Klarik, and the softer
Scandinavian model. There, the exemplar is Copenhagen's Zastrup airport, which
has the unique distinction of having been largely built through all its phases from
the 1930s to today mostly by one firm of architects, Vilhelm Lauritzen. So fond
are the Danes of the original 1936–9 Lauritzen terminal, with its rope-
balustraded spiral stairs and undulating roof, that when it became redundant and
was threatened with demolition as the airport expanded in the 1990s the
building was saved. The entire structure was stripped, sliced from its foundations

All pictures Vilhelm Lauritzen designed one of the best pre-war airport terminals. Copenhagen's Zastrup of 1936–9 is organic-modern in feel. It was recently restored for private use.

and moved on low-loaders 3.8km (more than 2 miles) to the far side of the airport over two days in September 1999, after which it was restored.

New York's La Guardia, although it quickly became congested, nonetheless showed that by 1939 America was catching up fast. Delano and Aldrich, by dint of working for Pan American, had gained wide experience of the type of buildings that would be needed by the newer generation of faster, larger planes – which meant up to 40 passengers, or as many as 75 in a flying boat, with speeds of up to 320kph (200mph). All this would, of course, be overturned by the arrival of large jet airliners after World War Two, but for a brief moment La Guardia was state of the art. It can even be said to anticipate the most common configuration of major airports by the start of the 21st century, since the main land-plane terminal divided arriving and departing passengers between two levels and led them via a glazed bridge to a spine concourse, 457m (1,500ft) long and curving to either side of the main building, reaching as far as the great hangars laid out on either side. As many as 24 planes at a time could dock at this spine. The notion of the departure gate was there, in the form of 11 'despatcher booths' placed at intervals along the concourse. The interiors of both terminals drew

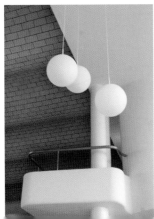

Above The land terminal at La Guardia, New York, shown here in 1946, was designed by Delano and Aldrich.

Opposite Flying boats were a vital part of America's air industry, seen here at Delano and Aldrich's Miami Dinner Key terminal in 1932. Note the extending walkways.

heavily on the domed rotundas to be found in the practice's other buildings. The interior of the land-plane terminal was dramatic indeed, with an impressive gilded frieze of the signs of the zodiac running around the dome and a giant globe hanging dead centre, both by interior designer Arthur Covey, to emphasize the international, nay cosmic, nature of the terminal. Like Tempelhof, but for different reasons, it also made use of the heraldic device of the eagle.

State of the art? As Delano himself said in 1950: 'It did not take long to discover that it was much too small and soon overcrowded, as it is today.' The terminal buildings were ridiculously tiny compared with Berlin, and the runway capacity was equally constrained. So La Guardia was the state of a very different art from Berlin's Tempelhof, which assumed massive growth in passenger numbers. It could not be said to represent the future for another reason since, like San Francisco and Miami, it was designed to accommodate planes arriving either on land or on water, with a wet and a dry terminal for each. This distinction was, in fact, blurred from the outset, because land planes could and did use the marine terminal, while a waterway inlet was provided to the land terminal, just in case. Both Americans and British were fond of the flying boat, but from the British point of view the preference was more to do with serving far-flung reaches of empire, because flying boats could carry more fuel, so had a greater range and could serve countries with no runways at all. America, with its huge potential domestic market, could have made the switch to wholly land-based airports sooner. Why did it not? Perhaps there was still that conviction, dating back to Langley and his disastrous 'aerodrome' experiments at the start of the century, that water was somehow safer (see page 32). It was certainly cheaper, but it was not necessarily as reliable as a runway, even when made extensively sheltered as it was off Bowery Bay at La Guardia. As it happened, developments

Above A short 'Caledonian' flying
boat of Imperial Airways cruises
over Manhattan.

Below André Lurcat's 1932 design
for a city-centre airport in Paris.

in plane technology during the forthcoming war would make the maritime side of La Guardia redundant, which is, paradoxically, why Delano and Aldrich's marine air terminal is the one building from that time to have survived.

All the inter-war phases of airport terminal design are still in use somewhere. Even André Lurcat's 1932 design for a 'relay airport' on an island in the River Seine right by the Eiffel Tower was not so illogical as it appeared, since this model was essentially adopted to convert a dockside quay surrounded by water into the London City airport in the 1980s, just as a clutch of skyscrapers was starting to be built at nearby Canary Wharf. Nor are earlier models yet defunct. At plenty of airports today – particularly the smaller ones used by budget airlines, but even at some relatively large new terminals – passengers still walk through a door and across the apron and climb the steps into the plane – often without even a canopy overhead, as provided so effectively by Sagebiel at Tempelhof. But the largest airports in the world at the start of the 21st century have largely reverted to the original Mendelsohnian idea of the single immense building performing all functions.

By the outbreak of World War Two civilian air travel was becoming much less of an ordeal. Le Corbusier had observed: 'Before 1930 you vomited in an aeroplane for two hours, for four hours … it was quite simply unbearable.' That from an enthusiast of flying and of the aeroplane as a functionalist object. Le Corbusier was talking about the era of the adapted World War One bomber. But in the 1930s purpose-designed airliners were looking forward to the planes of today rather than back to the 'stringbag' days. By the end of the decade, people were flying in large, comfortable Douglases, Boeings, Lockheeds, capacious Armstrong Whitworths, fast Italian Savoia-Marchettis, British De Havillands and Japanese Nakajimas, an assortment of big flying boats from Boeing, Short and Sikorsky and, perhaps the most luxurious airliner of the time, the Focke-Wulfe Condor. This degree of comfort was now matched by the terminal buildings themselves, which had undergone a similar transformation during the decade. From their beginnings in the 1920s they had rapidly evolved into a new building type. But in the meantime, another strand of airport design was continuing. Utopianists and visionaries had always seen them in different, more romantic, terms, as episodes in an urban dream. These, as the next chapter relates, are the airports that existed only on paper.

Above Interior architecture applied to France's giant 'Rochambeau' flying boat, 1939, as shown in the bar on the Paris-New York run.

Right The future, in the inter-war period, lay in the new breed of fast, comfortable land planes. This is the hugely successful Douglas DC-3 'Dakota', as operated by Sabena airline in 1936.

chapter three

From the first the possibilities of manned flight excited the attention of architects and utopianists. If Modernism was all about the machine age, the aeroplane logically represented the peak of technological achievement. Architects such as Le Corbusier (1887–1965) and Frank Lloyd Wright (1867–1959), who were avid motorists, also looked to the skies for inspiration, albeit in very different ways. In Le Corbusier's case the functionalist aesthetic of the machines themselves influenced his early architecture – his writings on ships, aircraft and cars make this explicit. With Wright it was an altogether subtler matter. Always opposed to the European Modernists, he ploughed his own furrow. The architect of the ground-hugging Prairie House designed no airport nor did he espouse mechanistic imagery. Yet his own utopian vision was informed by the possibilities of flight. His drawings for Broadacre City, the low-rise, urban idyll that was in direct contrast to the high-rise city dreams of Le Corbusier, depict the inhabitants flitting around in extraordinary Wright-designed autogyros, like individual flying saucers with rotor blades on top.

Chapter Three The Romantic Illusion

Like Henry Ford, Wright held on longer than most to the flawed notion that flight could be an individual thing – that people could strap on their wings like Icarus – but then, the imagery was all that preoccupied him. Despite his love of motoring, the cars that Wright also designed for Broadacre City in its last iteration in 1958 were as impracticable as his flying machines. Henry Ford could have pointed out to him that a four-wheeled car with the wheels quixotically arranged in diamond formation – two huge ones at either side, two little ones to front and rear – was inherently unstable, just as Igor Sikorsky could have explained that a flying saucer with a rotor on top, like Leonardo's helicopter sketch, would have spun round in the air like a centrifuge. These things did not concern Wright. He merely saw the decorative potential of the circular and domed shapes he was incorporating into virtually all of his buildings at that late stage of his career. He clung to the idea of freedom of suburban individuals with their house, their acre of land, their car and their plane, in direct contrast to the centralized cities proposed by the European urbanists.

Broadacre City was a project that occupied Wright at intervals from the early 1930s until his death. He was all in favour of zoning certain activities, but he always resisted the idea of an airport. His little personal helicopters, which he called 'aerotors', had taken their place in the Broadacre plans exhibited in 1935. This was four years before Sikorsky – then best known for his Clipper flying boats – was to make the first serious helicopter flight. The prospect of the new technology allowed Wright to imagine his aerotors as taking over from planes with their inconvenient need for long, space-hungry landing fields. This would conveniently allow them to land on the open terraces of his houses. Convenient, because the whole rationale of Broadacre City was to avoid centralized facilities – so there was no single dominant industry, no cultural quarter, no railroad station, no airport (though he was gradually to admit some collective functions such as a university). It was effectively an organizing hand placed on the natural phenomenon of suburban sprawl. In this, as with so much else, Wright was ahead of his time in anticipating the Edge City, the Technoburb. And when it came to flight, he got it wrong.

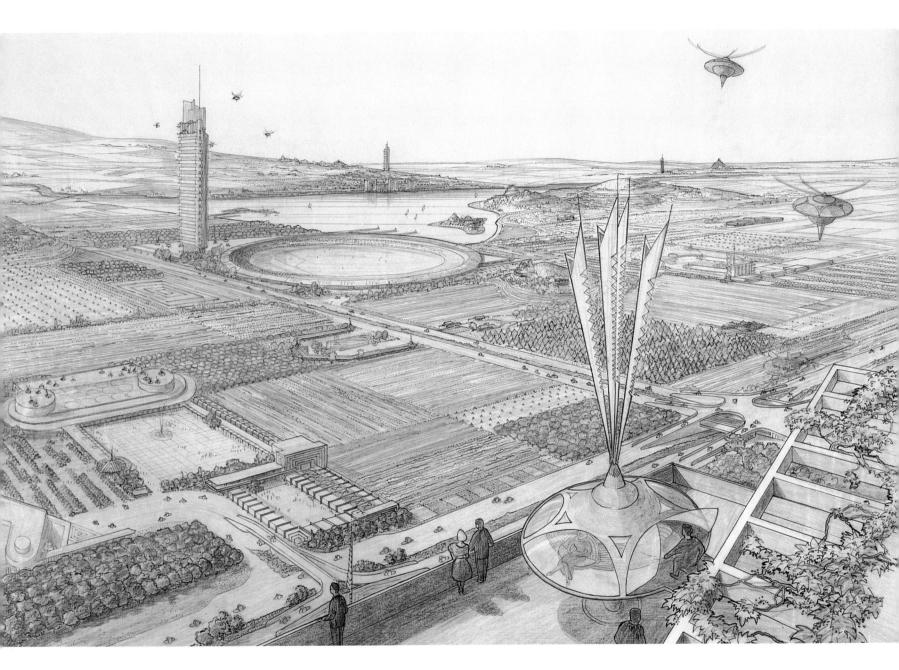

Above Frank Lloyd Wright's 'aerotors'
hover over Broadacre City in the
1950s version of an earlier design.
The idea was that each traveller had a
personal aircraft, so no centralized
airport was needed.

Previous The 'Armstrong Seadrome'.

Above Landing between skyscrapers – Le Corbusier adapted his Ville Contemporaine city-central airport design in the Plan Voisin shown here (1922–5). It was appropriately named after and sponsored by the aircraft maker, Voisin.

'Each citizen of the future will have all forms of production, distribution, self improvement, enjoyment, within a radius of a hundred and fifty miles of his home now easily and speedily available by means of his car and his plane,' wrote Wright in *The Disappearing City* (1932). 'This integral whole composes the great city that I see embracing all of this country – the Broadacre City of tomorrow.'

What actually happened, as we now know with the benefit of hindsight, was that passenger planes not only awkwardly continued to require airfields of their own but that those airfields became steadily larger, fewer in number and more remote from the cities and regions they served, in direct contradiction to Wright's (and Henry Ford's and the great inventor/engineer Buckminster Fuller's) vision of the personal, unregulated aircraft for everyone. And whereas baby helicopters and tiny planes are indeed today owned and flown by some wealthy private individuals from their well-spaced homes, just as Wright envisaged, the catastrophic implications of a city full of them, all getting in each others' way was not a thought he wished to entertain. Still, it was the imagery that counted, and it struck a chord with successive generations of architects. The enduring image of the early plan of Britain's 1960s grid-plan new town, Milton Keynes, is the Helmut Jacoby aerial perspective with helicopter in foreground.

For Richard Buckminster Fuller (1895–1983) the impossible dream was to design and build a vehicle that could operate on land and water and in the air. A flavour of the thinking can be seen in his 1928 sketches for the 4D Auto-Airplane, with three hydraulic engines and pneumatically sprouting wings. This all eventually boiled down to the delightful if unstable teardrop-shaped Dymaxion three-wheeled car, one of which was briefly owned by the conductor Leopold Stokowski. The nearest Fuller ever got to his dream was his own stubby, car-like, amphibian seaplane. But all such exercises underline the fact that in America at this time there was still uncertainty about how aviation was going to evolve and what infrastructure would be needed to serve it. In Europe, with its network of post-World War One airfields, there was no such uncertainty about the viability of commercial flight – but there was still plenty of room for confusion over the best architectural solution.

In contrast to the American visionaries, Le Corbusier was accustomed to the tighter regulations and scarcer land of Europe and was always clear that the future lay in aircraft as a means of public rather than private transport. There in his design for the Ville Contemporaine (1922), with its 3 million inhabitants, is the central transport interchange so conspicuously lacking from Wright's later Broadacre City. As with Antonio Sant'Elia's earlier Futurist proposal (see page 82), it is logical but flawed: a layer-cake of roads, mainline railway and metro lines, topped with an airfield (he has a motorway running right underneath it) and surrounded by the characteristic early-Corbusian forest of cruciform skyscrapers. The critic Peter Reyner Banham scoffed at the perils inherent in this plan, as with Sant'Elia's. As it turned out, the scary prospect of planes landing among skyscrapers was to become a reality in some parts of the world – it happened for years at Hong Kong's old airport and to some extent still does at others, such as London City, where departing planes fly straight towards the clustered towers of the Canary Wharf financial district before peeling off to left or right. Le Corbusier's and Pierre Jeanneret's perspective drawings of the Ville

Contemporaine do make flight look a bit scary, with large biplanes approaching the centre at vertiginous angles.

The principal problem was not so much the proximity of skyscrapers as the lack of space on the airfield itself. As with Agache's Canberra 'Aerostatic Station' competition design of 1912 (see page 40), Le Corbusier's airfield was landlocked. It could not grow. But Le Corbusier learned. He was to correct this error by the time of his Ville Radieuse plan (1930), in which he pushed the airport and transport zone to the outskirts, chiding himself: 'Any concentrically designed city (all cities created in the past on ground plans determined by "donkey tracks", also my own 1922 project for a modern city of 3 million inhabitants) makes regular, organic development impossible: a biological defect.' In theory the Ville Radieuse was, like Broadacre City, infinitely expandable, unlike other utopias with distinct perimeters.

The lure of the plane for Le Corbusier was explicit. He worshipped it as he worshipped the ship and the automobile. In his essay 'Airplanes' in *L'Esprit Nouveau* (1920), he wrote: 'The airplane is indubitably one of the products of the most intense selection in the range of modern industry. The War was an insatiable client, never satisfied, always demanding better. The orders were to succeed at all costs and death followed a mistake remorselessly. We may then affirm that the airplane mobilized invention, intelligence and daring: imagination and cold reason. It is the same spirit that built the Parthenon.'

Sprinkling his text with photographs of Farmans, Blériots, Spads and the extraordinary Caproni triple-biplane flying boat, intended to carry 100 passengers, Le Corbusier elaborated his theme – that 'architects have been asleep' while real progress in lean design was taking place elsewhere. 'Paris to Prague in six hours … Paris to Warsaw in nine hours … London to Paris in two hours', run the captions beneath his favourite plane, the Farman Goliath. All this he took as necessary support for his emerging theories of the house as a machine for living in, though at this stage he did not state that aphorism.

His conclusions are, as one might expect from this contradictory personality, somewhat eccentric. That he recommended a gramophone, pianola or wireless in every house on the grounds that 'you will avoid catching cold in the concert hall, and the frenzy of the virtuoso' says much about his and his clients' assumed position in the social hierarchy, as does his directive: 'Demand that the maid's room should not be an attic. Do not park your servants under the roof.' Finally, he returns to architecture and how it could gain from aircraft technology: 'Every modern man has the mechanical sense. The feeling for mechanics exists and is justified by our daily activities. This feeling in regard to machinery is one of respect, gratitude and esteem. Machinery includes economy as an essential factor leading to minute selection. There is a moral sentiment in the feeling for mechanics. The man who is intelligent, cold and calm has grown wings to himself. Men – intelligent, cold and calm – are needed to build the house and to lay out the town.'

Cold and calm was not how one would characterize the fevered rhetoric of the Italian Futurists as led by artist Umberto Boccione and architect F.T. Marinetti. The dramatic drawings of Antonio Sant'Elia, so influential on the end-of-the-century work by architects such as Richard Rogers and Renzo Piano, evoke the

Above The side view of the transport hub of Antonio Sant'Elia's La Città Nuova of 1914.

Opposite Sant'Elia's airport and transport interchange.

Overleaf An engraving of New York's Grand Central Station in 1876. The interchange inspired a generation of airport designers.

romance of the industrial society rather than its intellectual or economic rationale. Sant'Elia's only surviving building, the modest, traditional and highly ornamented Villa Elisi (1912) above Lake Como, gives no clue to his thinking at that time. Great towering cityscapes were forming in his mind and on his sketchpad. Power stations and dams intrigued and excited him. He signed up to the Futurist glorification of industrialized, speed-defined Modernism, although he quickly modified his position by setting up the calmer Nuove Tendenze group in 1913. He reached what – in view of his tragically short life – may be regarded as his creative peak over four months in 1914. In this period he designed, exhibited and published his perspective drawings for La Città Nuova. Of the 16 Sant'Elia drawings displayed in the Nuove Tendenze exhibition that opened in Milan on 20 May 1914, the key ones for our purposes are those subtitled 'Station for airplanes and trains'.

Sant'Elia's thinking, as contained in his catalogue essay 'Messagio', is pegged to the high-octane Futurist vision of an entirely new beginning, and uses characteristic Futurist rhetoric: 'We shall sing of the great crowds galvanized by labour, pleasure or unrest: of the many-coloured and polyphonic tides of revolution in the modern capitals; we shall sing of the vibrating nocturnal fervour of the arsenals and the building yards ablaze with violent electric moons; of swollen railway stations, avid for smoking serpents; of factories hung from the clouds by means of the twisted arabesques of their smoke; of bridges bestriding rivers like giant gymnasts … of bold steamboats scouting the horizons, of broad-chested locomotives pawing the tracks like huge steel horses bridled with pipes, and the gliding flight of airplanes.'

There is no doubt that the language is a great deal more entertaining than Le Corbusier's later dry analyses. And when it came to enshrining this vision in drawings, Sant'Elia does not let us down. La Città Nuova is not concerned so much with individual buildings as with infrastructure. His 'station for airplanes and trains' knots the transport routes into one great layered megastructure. He was much concerned with transport design, having two years previously unsuccessfully entered a competition for a new Milan railway terminus. His imagined earth-air station is wholly defined by its transport arteries, but we are given no clue as to how it would look inside. It is stratified, its many levels linked by elevators and escalators, which serve to define the monumental sloping glass façade of the huge building with its four slender rectangular towers. And beyond this great transverse terminal building, aligned precisely on axis between the towers, an airstrip stretches off into the middle distance, hemmed in at the sides by indicated buildings but with its end disappearing towards the horizon. Large biplanes are roughly indicated, like giant dragonflies.

Sant'Elia drew on a number of sources for this work, not least pre-World War One studies for multi-layered cities in the United States. These, however, while separating traffic flows, had not gone the extra step and considered the implications of air travel. Even the most influential of them all, Charles Lamb's 1908 designs for a new stratified New York with great high-level bridges spanning between skyscrapers, skated over this issue. Various versions of Lamb's scheme appeared, most notably in the plagiarized *King's Dream of New York*,

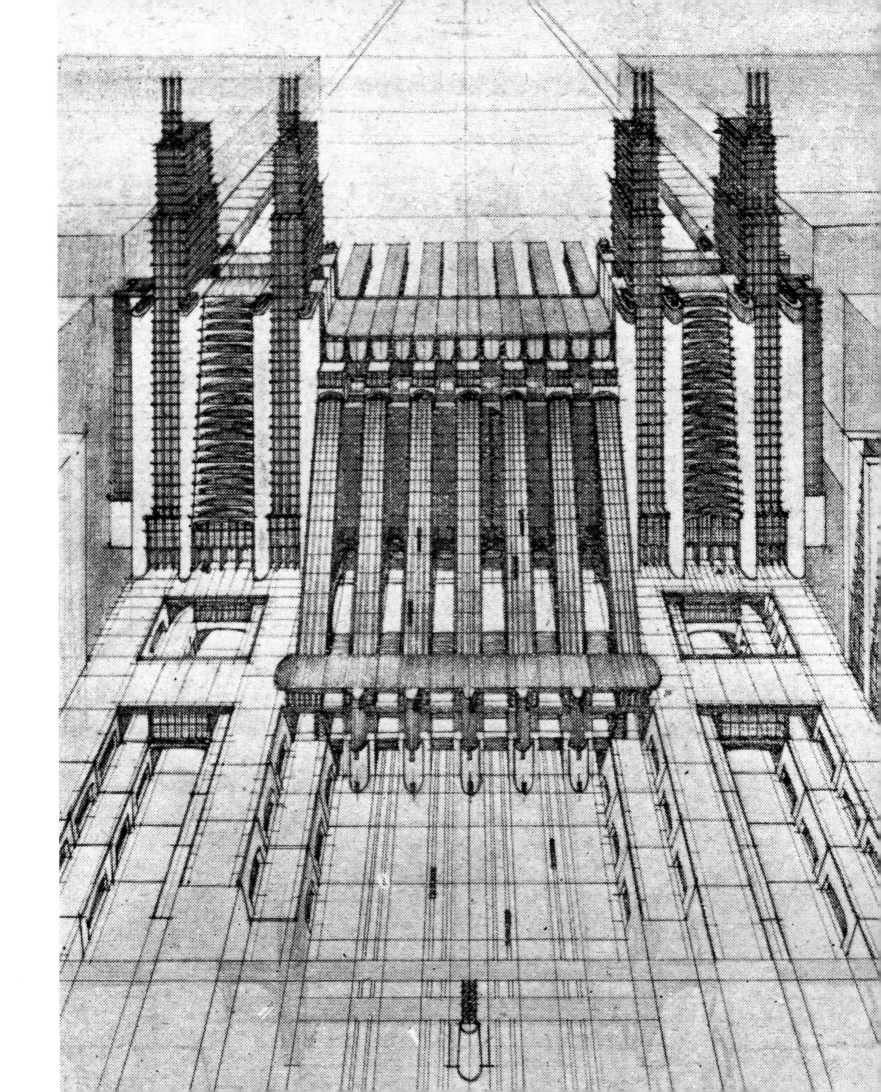

also published in 1908, where illustrator Harry Petit depicted the skies above Lamb's future metropolis filled with both dirigibles and heavier-than-air craft, without giving any clue as to where or how they were to land.

Sant'Elia's biographer, Esther da Costa Meyer, suggests that as well as these earlier studies, contemporary Milanese plans for huge highways slicing through the historic fabric of the fast-expanding industrial city may have given the young architect the visual stimulus for his mighty rooftop runways. For the terminal building itself, he points to the influence of cutaway sections of New York's Grand Central Station by Reed, Stern, Warren and Wetmore (considered also in the introduction to this book as a precursor of modern air terminal design, see page 16) published in Italy in 1912. These drawings depicted the sophisticated layering of transport and pedestrian routes at Grand Central that continue to work flawlessly today. It is certainly true that these images were current at the time Sant'Elia was designing La Città Nuova. His great leap forward was to unite such current ideas with the idea of air travel and to propose a workable solution to the handling of aircraft.

Consequently we can consider the 'Station for airplanes and train' of La Città Nuova as an astonishingly prescient design for its time. In its complexity and ambition it far exceeded Mendelsohn's sketches of the same period (see page 36). Its failings at first glance appear clear enough from our perspective 90 years later – most notably the relatively confined space indicated for planes to operate from. But looking at Sant'Elia's tantalizingly few drawings and sketches, one begins to wonder if he got it quite so wrong and if Banham was quite so right to dismiss the scheme. In one sketch there are indicated buildings – wings stretching out from the back of the main terminal to either side of the runway – that would or could incorporate hangars and maintenance workshops. His aerial perspectives suggest that this urban megastructure could be infinitely extrudable – so the runway could, in theory, be lengthened as required. As for the problem of planes flying into towers, they are kept relatively low – certainly no higher than many a control tower at a modern airport – and Sant'Elia is careful to space them widely, allowing a clear flight path between them. True, the definition of the runway strip was all wrong for the needs of the light aircraft of the time, which needed to be able to take off into the wind in any direction – hence the generally circular or square shape of most real airfields of the day. But Sant'Elia was thinking for the future. All in all, the plan is a great deal more pragmatic than might at first appear, particularly when we remember that no commercial passenger aviation services were at that time in operation, (apart from Zeppelin's airships in Germany), and that Sant'Elia's drawings suggest heavier-than-air craft, and so this design was absolutely starting from scratch. Given this, the wonder is not how much he got wrong, but how much he got right.

What makes the scheme so interesting to modern eyes is its sheer scale and complexity. As we have already noted, the buildings actually in existence serving aviation at that time were little more than big sheds and – for the viewing public – grandstands derived from racecourses. So it took a great leap of the imagination to design a future city that not only assumed the existence of passenger air travel but also assumed huge numbers of people using air transport, arriving by a variety of means and being efficiently processed through a broadly rectangular building aligned transversely so as to leave the shortest possible distance between arrival and departure. Despite Sant'Elia's dislike of boring plans and his love instead of the spectacular perspective, that much is clear. Given which – and given how far his own architecture had come in a very short time – his death in 1916 on the mountainous Italian front at the age of 28 was doubly tragic. His last known piece of design was the military cemetery in which he himself was to be buried. Even that does not survive; it was destroyed in 1917.

There is obviously no knowing what kind of real airport Sant'Elia might have designed had he survived to see the step-change in aviation technology that the war brought about and to which Le Corbusier was to refer. Perhaps he would have been caught up in the increasingly fascistic tendencies of the Futurists, whose overblown and violently worded manifesto, drafted by Marinetti, was published with his name attached earlier in 1916. He was certainly posthumously evoked by the Futurists in support of their pro-fascist, anti-Semitic stance – on no evidence at all, it would appear, beyond his patriotism in the war. Whatever his politics, there is no doubt he could have contributed enormously to the development of civil aviation. As it is, the Città Nuova drawings survive as the earliest workable depiction of a modern, architect-designed airport terminal, a fantastical dream grounded in hard thinking that was, in several important respects, to become reality by the close of the 20th century.

There were to be many other attempts to pin down the ideal airport with its associated buildings. The almost constant human activity of designing utopias was greatly stimulated around the start of the 20th century by the arrival of widespread electrical power. The new utopias made full use of this wonder power source, not least because it allowed swift and clean means of public transport. As with Sant'Elia, the technological utopias were defined by their transport networks, and these increasingly included planes and skyscrapers in the now familiar if slightly alarming combination.

As early as 1900, visions of a future Manhattan were being informed by the existence of airships. In the *New York World* magazine of 30 December that year, an illustrator named Biedermann imagined a densely packed city of skyscrapers 99 years hence. Apart from the fact that his illustration includes not one but two prophetic pairs of twin towers in Lower Manhattan – one tapering pair curiously reminiscent of the Petronas towers that Cesar Pelli was to build in the 1990s in Kuala Lumpur – the big idea was rectangular landing strips on the roofs of lower, squatter towers. Biedermann was to return to his theme in 1916 with a far more elaborate transport system in the sky, including huge steel-truss landing platforms for all kinds of flying machines.

Similarly, Herman Brinsmade's Utopia Achieved (1912) draws on the imagery of Charles Lamb's multi-level New York of 1908 with its bridge-linked skyscrapers and depicts planes of one kind or another flitting with ease among them. Brinsmade's solution to the problem of where to land planes in a vertical city is suggested by his illustrations of hybrid aircraft with vertical landing capability. From the top of one of his neoclassical skyscrapers rises a pylon supporting what looks very like a modern helicopter pad, with a large biplane perched on top of it. This proved to be an enduring image, both in utopian

Below A 1908 science-fiction dream of a New York inhabited by aircraft.

Opposite The dream was still alive in 1928, as shown in this illustration for Earl L. Bell's *The Moon Doom*, from *Amazing Stories* magazine in 1928.

PASSENGER AND FREIGHT DIRIGIBLES AND AIRPLANES USING AIRPORTS ON ROOF OF BUILDING.

CITY OF FUTURE TO BE SINGLE UNIT OF REINFORCED CONCRETE FACED WITH BRONZE AND GLASS, ABOUT 1,000 FEET HIGH WITH 15 TIMES THE FLOOR AREA OF THE WOOLWORTH BUILDING. THIS STRUCTURE WOULD HOUSE ABOUT 150,000 PEOPLE.

DIRIGIBLE MASTS

AIRPLANE LANDING FIELDS

BUILDING IN CENTER OF 20-MILE SQUARE METROPOLITAN DISTRICT, LAND BEING TAKEN UP WITH FARMS, FOREST AND PARKS, ALL EASILY ACCESSIBLE WITHIN FIVE MINUTES' RUN FROM BUILDING.

ALL ROOMS HAVE UNOBSTRUCTED VIEW OF SURROUNDING COUNTRY, BEING COLUMNATED WITH BRONZE-BUTTRESSED GLASS WINDOWS, REFLECTING LIGHT TO ALL PARTS OF STRUCTURE. BY MEANS OF SYSTEM OF BLINDS, LIGHT CAN BE SHUT OFF AT WILL

RESIDENTIAL, ADMINISTRATION, AND AMUSEMENTS

LANDING STATIONS AND DISTRIBUTION

INDUSTRIALS IN FOUNDATION AND LOWER STORIES.

FORTY ACRE BUILDING ERECTED ON FLOATING FOUNDATION OF CAISSONS IN A RESERVOIR OF LIQUID MUD AS PROTECTION FROM TORNADOS QUAKES, ETC.

LLOYD WRIGHT

thinking and in science-fiction magazines. In 1928 a Frank R. Paul illustration in the magazine *Amazing Stories* returns to the Lamb-Brinsmade model of a high-rise technopolis interlaced with multi-level bridges. Paul expands Brinsmeade's single-plane landing platform into a large rectangular landing field in the sky, supported like a table on corner towers culminating in steel pylons. So that this does not cast the city below into shadow, it is depicted as being somehow transparent, an optimistic anticipation perhaps of the use of structural glass.

By the 1920s serious architects and planners were appropriating this fanciful imagery. A 1926 design by Lloyd Wright (son of Frank and, in the normal course of events, a good architect completely eclipsed by his father) is for a 305m (1,000ft) earthquake-proof, cruciform supertower in Los Angeles: a vertical city, a skyscraper utopia. It looks suspiciously like one of Le Corbusier's towers of 1922, but inflated to superscale. Wright may have had his tongue in his cheek – this was a publicity-seeking exercise in the *Los Angeles Examiner* – but he had it all worked out, wrong.

This reinforced concrete, bronze-and-glass-clad megatower would house 150,000 people and would be served by 'passenger and freight dirigibles and airplanes using airports on roof of building'. The illustration shows how this was to be achieved, and it is madder than anything previously proposed. Wright Jr envisaged a multi-storey runway structure perched on top of the tower, in which a dozen landing fields – cruciform, like the tower below them, but slightly oversailing its edges – are stacked one above the other. Somehow or other planes would have to dive in the narrow slots between each level. How the weight of all these slabs would be supported and still allow enough clear space for the planes to land is not divulged. All one can say about the design is that the cruciform layout was a sound one to allow take-off and landing in different directions. Wright did not, however, carry this thinking through to his airship mooring masts on top, for they are arranged so as to allow the airships to point in only one direction. If the wind changed, fearful collisions would result.

Lloyd Wright was only one of many. In the early 1920s skyscraper architect Harvey Wiley Corbett and the perspective artist Hugh Ferris began to collaborate on a series of studies – initially sparked by the way New York's zoning laws allowed set-back skyscrapers – that culminated in their proposal for Titan City. They excitedly used the mandatory planning set-backs to create broad, elevated terraces – linked, of course, by high-level bridges. And, of course, they put aircraft landing platforms on the tops of the skyscrapers.

London was to consider such a rooftop airport proposal as late as 1931, by which time it had become clear that if any such proposal were to succeed, it would have to incorporate many buildings. There is a pleasing logic to architect Charles Glover's radial airport-in-the-sky proposal of that year for London's King's Cross district. First, he was adding air travel to an existing heavily used transport interchange – the equivalent of New York's Penn Station. Second, he recognized that aircraft needed both a reasonable length of runway – at that time 800m (½ mile) was considered sufficient – and the ability to take off in any direction. Hence the radial pattern, and circular perimeter for taxi-ing purposes. Finally, he took the crucial step of suggesting the construction of a whole network of buildings to support an airfield of sufficient size.

The result was like an immense spoked wheel. London at that time had no skyscrapers, so there would have been clear approach and take-off paths for planes from any direction. The plan made a great deal more sense than Le Corbusier's 1922 idea of a centralized airport, which, as we have seen, Le Corbusier himself was shortly to renounce (see page 81). Glover made a relatively detailed model of his proposal, indicated that passengers would rise to the departure level in lifts and that planes would similarly be raised from below as with aircraft carriers. The elevated circular plan would have made it difficult, if not impossible, to lengthen the runways at a future date. Of course, if a plane were to overshoot the runway catastrophe would result, but for all that, the scheme was a brave late attempt to centralize an airport and incorporate it into the city fabric.

It was not the last such attempt. Even by 1945, with a fresh wartime experience of large-runway construction to refer to, some British architects still yearned for the impossible dream. In that year architects Kenneth Lindy and Winton Lewis, as part of a set of proposals for rebuilding the blitzed City of London financial district, designed a cruciform airport in the sky set on five new skyscrapers over another mainline station, Liverpool Street. Actually this was not so daft, for Lindy and Lewis had picked up on Sikorsky's invention of the helicopter, which they saw as the ideal passenger vehicle for places such as the City where land was scarce and expensive. Various subsequent plans for a City of London heliport were to continue until the 1990s before finally being killed off on grounds of noise. The Bell Helicopter Corporation continued to produce beguiling images of city-centre vertical-take-off-and-landing (VTOL) airports using a succession of its tilt-rotor aircraft designs right up to the end of the 20th century. It found itself in much the same position that the Curtiss-Wright company had in the 1920s – having to design the ground infrastructure for its technology, the difference being that Curtiss had real planes coming off the production lines while Bell had nothing but ideas and prototypes. Although small Bell tilt-rotor craft went into production, these did not amount to a seismic shift in aviation. The Bell city airport imagery – which returned to the idea of airports on top of transport interchanges – remained images only.

So true city-centre airports were not to be. Berlin's Tempelhof airport, so fortuitously close to the centre, was the nearest any European capital city ever came to that ideal until the 1980s, when the arrival of short-take-off-and-landing (STOL) passenger planes, such as small De Havilland turboprops and 'whisper jets', allowed relatively central former industrial and dockland areas to be converted into commuter airports in a number of European and US cities. Runways needed to be no longer than 1,200m (4,000ft) for the jets, and only 915m (3,000ft) for the turboprops, and relatively narrow. In contrast, a conventional heavy-airliner runway at the start of the 21st century was of concrete 3,700m (more than 12,000ft) long and 60m (nearly 200ft) wide, together with all the proportional run-off and runway separation space. Not only are such airports not possible in cities – they are themselves city-scale.

The romanticized idea of how flight and tall buildings could be combined was to permeate the 20th century in film, from *Things to Come* (1936) to *Blade Runner* (1982), in books and magazines, and in the dreams of architectural

Opposite The continuing dream of the airport in the sky. The City of London design for a development of Liverpool Street station, complete with gyro-plane landing platform, by Lindy and Lewis, dates from 1945.

Overleaf An elevated airport for London. This proposal for King's Cross by Charles Glover, 1931, aimed to add air travel to an existing interchange where aeroplanes could land on the runways of a huge wheel-shaped structure.

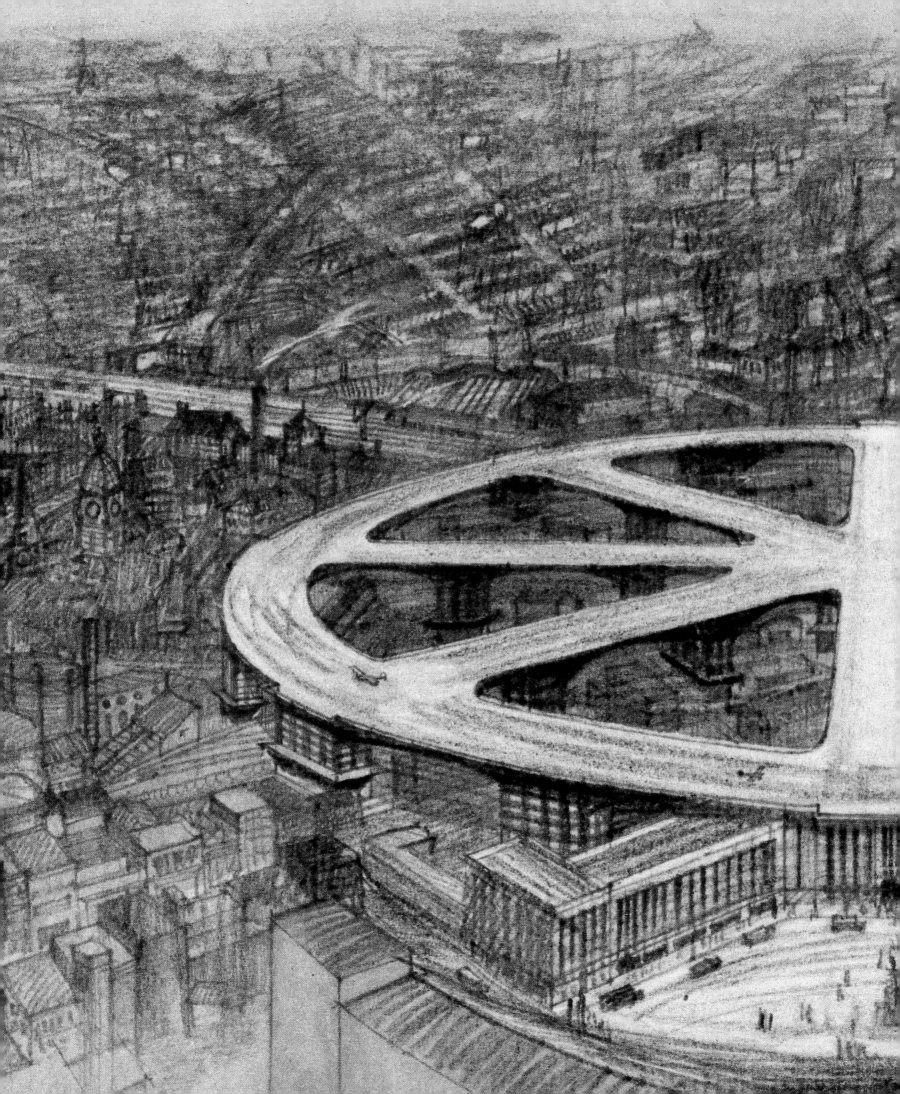

visionaries, such as Archigram in the 1960s. The tall building with flying machines circling it became one of the great clichés of architectural and fantasy thought: romantic but wrong. In reality, this pervasive idea was realized only in the form of helicopter pads, either on top of, or cantilevered out from, tall buildings, as with Norman Foster's Hong Kong and Shanghai Bank headquarters (1979–86), with its heroic helicopter platform. Set in the midst of this extraordinary skyscraper cityscape, it is one of the few real buildings that successfully alludes directly to the futuristic dreams of the early 20th century.

Sometimes, however, the blue-sky thinking got as far as serious practical studies. Making the transatlantic crossing from Europe to North America, for instance, exercised the minds of many. Despite the first nonstop flight by Alcock and Brown from Newfoundland to Ireland in their converted Vickers Vimy bomber in 1919 and Lindbergh's longer range mission to Paris in 1927, passenger planes just did not have the range to cover the distance. Even when it became possible, it was not comfortable – particularly when bad weather blew up. Lindbergh's plane, *The Spirit of St Louis*, was a Ryan monoplane modified to be a flying fuel tank: half of its take-off weight was fuel. There could be gasoline or passengers, but not both – not yet. One solution to this problem was current in various forms between the wars – floating airstrips in the sea.

The most fully worked-up example of these was the proposal for the 'Armstrong Seadrome', essentially a giant moored aircraft carrier, 365m (1,200ft) long by about 110m (350ft) wide, with hangars placed below deck. Positioned strategically at intervals across the Atlantic, the seadromes would not only have allowed otherwise short-range planes to progress from continent to continent in short hops, but would also have provided the kind of emergency back-up routinely provided along land-based routes. The Curtiss-Wright company was busy building a string of small, short-hop airports and proposed this as the model for the entire nation. The US Postal Service and most early airlines maintained emergency strips as well as their scheduled stopping and refuelling points. To an extent this is still true today: a number of basic airports around the world are kept in business purely because they are needed in case of emergency landings. The seadrome was a logical extension of this thinking – do the same thing but out at sea, and true intercontinental flight would become possible.

Edward Armstrong, a Canadian-American engineer, started designing his seadrome as early as 1913. To be stable, it had to be big – originally 50,800 tonnes (50,000 tons) displacement, with a deck 335m (1,100ft) long and a draft of 55m (180ft). Inside this huge hull would be not only maintenance and refuelling workshops for the planes, but also all the facilities of an air terminal, including a 40-room hotel. For added stability, it would be tethered to the sea floor. This was not an idle notion. Armstrong got the Roebling Company, inventors of wound steel cable and suspension bridge pioneers (they built the Brooklyn Bridge), to devise a deep-water anchoring system for him.

Seadromes almost happened. Over the years Armstrong accumulated backers for his scheme. One was about to start construction – it is not recorded at what point in the Atlantic – in early 1930, but in October 1929 the New York stock market crashed, the Great Depression followed, and the Seadrome was fatally

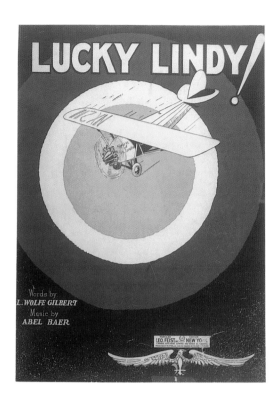

Above A 1927 music sheet cover
illustrates a popular song entitled
'Lucky Lindy!', which makes reference
to Lindbergh's transatlantic flight.

Previous The 'Armstrong Seadrome'
was a fully-engineered proposal
for tethered relay stations across
the Atlantic.

delayed. In 1934 Armstrong got the ear of President Roosevelt and it was briefly
back on the national agenda, but by then Zeppelins were providing a nonstop
transatlantic passenger service. Seadromes would have helped the Allied war
effort, but they would have been obvious targets for U-boats. By the 1940s
heavier-than-air planes had the necessary range to make the idea obsolete.

But it is not obsolete. Floating airports are once more being touted as a
solution to scarce land resources and a scaled-down airport, 1,000m (3,280ft)
long and 121m (400ft) wide, called Mega-Float, was built and successfully
tested in Tokyo Bay in 2000. Tests showed that a version four times the size was
eminently feasible.

By the end of World War Two architects and designers took leave of the
science-fiction magazine illustrators with whom they had shared so much for
more than two decades. The mood was already changing before the war.
Designer Norman Bel Geddes (1893–1958), famous for streamlined cars,
predicted an automobile-dominated future at the New York World's Fair of
1939–40, but with an eye to future aviation too. The Fair was dedicated to
future-gazing in all its aspects (the year 1960 being the date its eyes were fixed
on). Bel Geddes was hired to design the Futurama pavilion, the most popular at
the Fair, which was sponsored by General Motors – hence the emphasis on the
highway. He had previously designed a succession of fantastical aircraft – mainly
huge flying-wing formation seaplanes culminating in the 20-engine, $9 million
Airliner Number 4 (1929), which was intended to rival ocean liners in its levels of
luxury, right down to its many decks, its huge dining room with orchestra and
(enclosed) games and promenade areas. Had it been built, it would have dwarfed
today's 747s and A380s. But by 1939 Bel Geddes had given up on the giant
seaplane idea and was designing for land planes. The Futurama pavilion
contained a fascinating illustration, 'Airport Tomorrow', showing a great circular
airport just across the river from the southern tip of Manhattan.

This was the new realism setting in. Bel Geddes, in selecting a by then old-
fashioned circular design, was making the classic futurologist's move as
recommended by H.G. Wells – simply taking the present and making it much
bigger rather than imagining anything significantly different. The days of the
circular airport were by then drawing to a close, but in its scale and location Bel
Geddes was much nearer the mark. As were the new designs for a Chicago
airport, driven by the rapid overcrowding of the Municipal airport. As early as
1909 the Plan of Chicago by Daniel H. Burnham and Edward H. Bennett had
suggested reclaiming land from Lake Michigan. In 1920, the city fathers began
to do just this, so creating Northerly Island. It was immediately earmarked as one
possible site for an airport. Other offshore locations were considered. There were
many competing schemes. Thoughts started to crystallize in 1930 at the Century
of Progress Expo, where architects Vorhees, Gimelin and Walker designed an
offshore airport with twin terminals, for land- and seaplanes, as La Guardia was
later to have. Indecision continued, but all the plans continued to be for an airport
in the water. In 1945 a further plan by engineers De Leuw, Cather and Company
with architect Andrew N. Rebori produced options for an airport built on newly
reclaimed land in the lake. Still designed for both land and sea take-offs, this had
a single terminal. Rebori's drawings of the scheme seem remarkably modern

Above Charles Lindbergh set off on his first solo flight across the atlantic on 20 May 1927. His plane, the 'Spirit of St Louis', was a flying gas tank. The challenge was to find ways to carry passengers as well as fuel.

Opposite Norman Bel Geddes imagines a New York airport of 1960, but it was with a 1930s outlook.

Below Son of Seadrome: the working prototype of 'Megafloat' is assembled in Tokyo Bay, 2000.

today, in everything except the radial runway configuration, which was still needed at the time. Like the designs by others for floating or rooftop airports, this was to have storage and maintenance hangars below ground. It was to be connected to Northerly Island by a causeway.

Value-engineered into a more conventional format, this is what essentially happened. Meigs Field airport, as it was called, was built on its own island in the lake in the post-war years. This was to be only another staging-post in Chicago's long march towards a world mega-airport, but it marked a highly significant moment. The romantic but wrong strand of airport design, going back nearly 50 years, had engaged at last with the pragmatics of how airports had actually evolved over those years with real planes and real people. The industry was now big enough to start to think more ambitiously. The offshore airport was the real shape of things to come. But this was by no means to exclude romance and metaphor. For some years, as luxury took over from simple necessity, the architecture of airport buildings was greatly influenced by the form of the aircraft themselves.

chapter four

When the young and idealistic architects and designers of Ireland's Office of Public Works sat down to sketch out the new Dublin airport terminal in the late 1930s, they were clear on one thing: this was the modern portal to a young nation, and its imagery must be entirely of the new Ireland, not of the old – whether that meant the legacy of British rule or a nostalgia for some mythical and heroic past. Starting with a blank sheet of paper and clearly aware of the writings of Le Corbusier, they set to work. The modern world was best epitomized by the latest generation of wonderful aeroplanes, and so the building would respond aesthetically to the design of the planes themselves.

In consequence, Dublin airport terminal (1937–41) emerged as a wholly convincing exercise in suiting the building to its activities. Built at what had originally been the World War One airbase of Collinstown, it opened for business when air traffic was necessarily constrained, despite Ireland's neutral wartime status. Of course, it was informed by the ocean-liner imagery of the moderne style and the whole early Modern Movement obsession with light and air. It had its observation and cafe decks, as did virtually all airports of the day. This was a place to come and watch the brand-new new Douglas DC3s of Aer Lingus (a state airline set up as recently as 1936 with a single De Havilland Dragon biplane) touch down and swing smartly around on the apron in front of the curving terminal with its central control tower. Dublin had two vital routes in the immediately pre-war years, operating from another airfield, to London and to Liverpool, the historic port of maritime embarkation. World War Two put paid to the London service, but all through the war, at some risk, the air link to Liverpool was maintained, which meant that two of the architecturally most interesting terminals of the day – Dublin and Liverpool Speke – continued their stylistic conversation. There is a preserved De Havilland biplane at Speke as a memory of those days.

Chapter Four   The Imagery of Flight

Right The Dublin airport building appears to have a cockpit and wings, as if permanently poised for flight.

Opposite Aerial view of Dublin airport (1937–41) shows the overt aeroplane plan.

Previous Dulles International airport, Washington, D.C. by Eero Saarinen.

Above An illustration from 1936 – well-wishers wave goodbye to travellers about to begin a long-distance flight.

Below Paris, Orly in the 1950s with its uptilted roof and raking struts.

By the time the new Dublin airport was on the drawing-boards, the late Art Deco of Speke was distinctly unfashionable. That decadent style was not for go-ahead Ireland with its lofty ideals. The young Office of Public Works team under architect Desmond Fitzgerald was inspired not so much by Le Corbusier, as, perhaps, by the sweeping lines of Mendelsohn and Chermayeff's iconic De la Warr Pavilion at Bexhill-on-Sea, Sussex, in the south of England, an exotic moment in streamlined architectural fashion completed in 1935. They also took their cue from the Bauhaus – or, if you prefer, the Arts and Crafts movement – and designed everything, down to the door handles, the cutlery in the restaurant and even the menu cards. Their designs were, in fact, far ahead of the technology or the passenger throughput of the airport as a whole. Not only were there very few routes to serve, but the airport was built with a grass landing-strip at a time when all other major airports of the world, civilian and military, were starting to turn to the paved runway as a necessary adjunct to the heavier and faster planes being introduced.

So the new Dublin terminal was punching above its weight, suggesting an operational sophistication that was not there. It stood on the cusp of two eras: at the very end of the period of 1930s heroic Modernism, and before the necessary rapid expansion of the post-war years. Although the original building, much altered, is still to be found as part of the arrivals sequence today, its period of pre-eminence lasted only 18 years. By 1959, following the usual pattern of explosive growth in passenger numbers, a second terminal was required. By then, Aer Lingus was flying Lockheed Constellations to America.

The Dublin terminal was largely overlooked at the time because of the war, which, apart from anything else, meant that the plans of the terminal were considered a state secret and not published until 1945, when the world had changed. Even today, when it is better known, it tends to be mentioned, like Bexhill, for its maritime imagery. But in fact the imagery is multivalent. The tiered decks can be read in terms of a ship and its square control tower as the ship's bridge, but there were also rounded, concrete, cantilevered wings on the top deck, and in the early days, when it was seen from above, the plan was evident. This plan – which incorporated the landscaped approach sequence as well as the building itself – is that of an aeroplane. The curving terminal building (in this instance curving away from the apron rather than embracing it as was more usual) formed the wings, and the control tower on top was the cockpit. The axial approach was laid out to suggest a fuselage and tail. The aesthetic intention was very direct: from the air, this place looked like a plane. This could have been banal, but for the fact that the shape of a plane in plan happens to be an excellent diagram of the movement of people through such an airport: arrival, dispersal along the wings, departure, all pointing in the correct direction. This approach was to be adopted on a vast scale in the late 1990s by Norman Foster with his Chek Lap Kok international airport in Hong Kong – again, its ground plan takes the form of a stylized aeroplane when seen from the air.

Perhaps the most perfect architectural response to the design of aircraft in the late 1930s was the charming little monoplane building of the Ramsgate Aerodrome, built outside this minor English Channel port in 1936–7 to the designs of David Pleydell-Bouverie. The architectural historian Wolfgang Voigt

Above Building and aeroplane in perfect harmony: Ramsgate Aerodrome, 1936–7, by David Pleydell-Bouverie.

wrote in 1996: 'Probably nowhere else did the playful melding of a seemingly simple airport with the image of an airplane succeed so perfectly.' He is right. Ramsgate stands for all the wide-eyed aeronautical optimism of the era, the more so, perhaps, since it has vanished (presumed demolished in the late 1960s when the aerodrome closed), and so we are spared seeing it in flaky, hideously altered old age as is the fate of several others of its generation. Nor was this little gem compromised by association with later buildings by its architect. Pleydell-Bouverie, of English aristocratic stock, erstwhile partner of noted Modernist Wells Coates and a member of the hugely influential MARS group of radical architects, was an early drop-out. He built little and on completion of the aerodrome emigrated to America when he was 26 years old. He appears to have spent the rest of his long life as a recluse, restoring a run-down ranch north of San Francisco. He died in 1994, aged 83.

All pictures The sheltering wing at
Elmdon airport in Birmingham,
1938–9, by Norman and Dawbarn.

This abandonment of a conventional architectural career was certainly not because of the reception of his building, which was widely admired and published. Architectural historian Gavin Stamp suggests that the monochrome photograph by Dell and Wainwright, published in the *Architectural Review* of 1937 and reproduced here, is 'one of the most arresting images of British architecture between the two world wars'. Stamp notes the carefully contrived placement in the picture of a high-wing Short 16 Scion Junior 16-seat monoplane – which, having been designed in 1934, was contemporary with the building. If we examine this composition, we find that the photographer has used perspective so that the plane's wing exactly matches the perceived length of the oversailing cantilevered roof of Pleydell-Bouverie's building and is arranged in exact parallel with it. The propeller blade of the plane points precisely towards the building's centre point – the cockpit of the control box (a tower it is not), with two uniformed figures standing on the roof deck in front of it. Sections of the folding glass doors of the building's airside façade are seen in the open position, demonstrating the building's openness and flexibility.

The *Architectural Review* explained in its condescending way that: 'In airport architecture, a comparatively new problem, the detailed requirements are constantly changing, so that complete flexibility of planning has become essential.' Pleydell-Bouverie's response to this requirement was to make a non-loadbearing curtain wall beneath the canopy, so that 27m (90ft) of the 46m (151ft) length of the building could be opened up to the airfield. This was more for the benefit of diners in the restaurant, who were thus enabled to spill out on to the terrace, than for any operational purpose. From the air the 'flying wing' shape of the building would mark it out as an airport, if less directly than the Dublin plan, but in the end, that admirable photographic image is the thing. Even more than Dublin, tiny, unimportant Ramsgate represents the culmination of a particular aesthetic.

Other airport terminals of the time had moved in this literalist direction. Birmingham's Elmdon (Birmingham) airport terminal of 1938–9, by architect Nigel Norman and engineer Sir Graham Dawbarn, possesses 15m (50ft) wing-canopies to either side of the round-nosed main structure. The idea was to provide shelter for passengers and baggage on their way out to one of two planes – typically the De Havilland Dragons, Rapides and Jupiters of the era, although larger planes were allowed for – drawn up beneath the canopies. The idea was thus the same as Sagebiel's Tempelhof of the same date but far smaller and arranged entirely differently. The Elmdon terminal, rather than being arranged parallel with the edge of the apron, as was the case with so many other European airports of the time, projected out into it at right angles, a peninsula into the airside. Square at the landside end, apsidal on the runway end and arranged on five storeys, this is a fat Mississippi steamboat of a building with wings attached – now a protected building and still in use at the vastly expanded Birmingham International airport, housing air traffic control and business charter offices. For that matter, the unusual architecture-engineering practice of Norman and Dawbarn, founded in 1934, still exists and continues to work in the aviation sector. Elmdon is an interesting precedent because it proposed a different model

All pictures Norman Foster's
Stansted airport (opposite), and the
aeroplane that surely inspired it
(below): the early 1930s Handley
Page HP42 at the now-obsolete
Croydon airport.

to the norms of the day, a model that was later to be taken up not in main terminal buildings, but in the piers sprouting from them, as in the later, early 21st-century phases of Charles de Gaulle airport in Paris.

However, Elmdon's canopied approach to the planes was one aspect of its design that could not be said to anticipate the future, unless, that is, the future in question was the now-familiar one of budget airlines that eschew airbridges and expect their passengers to walk across the tarmac to the planes. On that scenario, perhaps the canopied airport terminal will make a comeback. But assuming not, a more prescient design than Elmdon, as we have seen, was the contemporary circular 'beehive' terminal at London Gatwick, with its radiating, telescopic walkways out to the planes. However, no beehive is that shape, even if some are circular. The original Gatwick terminal – more a flying saucer, in the days before flying saucers became the stuff of film fantasy – could be seen as an aviation-inspired design from the air, when its circular form, central boss and radiating spokes would read very much like the universally used radial aero-engines of the time with their curved cowlings. Perhaps it is fanciful to suggest that architects Hoar, Marlow and Lovett consciously modelled their Gatwick building on the form of, say, a Wright Cyclone engine (the Rolls-Royce Trent of its day), but the intriguing possibility is there.

So the aeronautical look took different forms. To achieve the look in the mainstream examples, it was necessary only to take the cue of the long, gently curved frontage with central control tower that had been evolving in airport buildings since the early German examples of the 1920s and to imbue that with the requisite symbolism. Usually the designers deployed the thin-shell concrete construction techniques that had been developing in the 1920s and 1930s, with cantilevered steelwork where necessary. The Elmdon building, being turned at right angles to the apron, was not planned that way and was more compact. Other airport configurations of the time, such as the impressive circular Helsinki-Malmi terminal (1938) by Dag Englund and Vera Rosendhal, were equally resistant to aeronautical imagery and so reverted to the related ship's bridge look.

It is perhaps curious that architects in the 1920s and 1930s did not pick up on the aerofoil-with-struts aesthetic of the early airliners, preferring instead the smooth white-Modern image. It was left to a later generation of high-tech architects to make the connection, and of the new generation of airports that emerged in the 1980s none does so more overtly than Norman Foster's Stansted, London's third airport and a huge influence on all subsequent terminal designs. Its importance as a planning diagram will be discussed fully in Chapter 6. Here, we are concerned with the way it looks, because the imagery of the architecture is inspired not by the planes of today, but by those of yesteryear.

Norman Foster, now Lord Foster, is, like several other architects of airports before him, a keen aviator. He is licensed to fly serious planes, not just little weekend flit-abouts. He waxes lyrical about the architectonic properties of the Boeing 747. Yet Stansted could not yield a photograph of the kind that Ramsgate did in the late 1930s, when plane and building were so plainly in harmony with each other. It is paradoxical that – for such a mould-breaking modern building – Stansted's visual references are, consciously or not, historicist. Its imagery is not of modern Boeings and Airbuses, but of Imperial Airways' Handley Page HP 42

Heracles class airliners of the early 1930s, with their oversailing top wings and sharply angled struts. Old-fashioned even when introduced, these stately 38-passenger, four-engined airliners, with their box-kite tailplanes, nonetheless connected the four corners of the British Empire at a maximum 160kph (100mph) and enjoyed a perfect safety record, not even registering any accidents. Imagine a breaker's yard of such airliners, filled with such wings and struts. Imagine setting them upright and joining them all together. The result would be like a junk model of Stansted, a building where the public concourses comprise an exceptionally light and lofty roof canopy composed of modules supported on 'trees' of braced steel struts. At the landside and airside edges, where the canopy oversails the curtain walls of the building to provide cover for road vehicles and automated transit trains respectively, the image is strikingly clear. In the almost obsessive functionalism and modularity of the Stansted design, there is room not only for beauty but also for nostalgia. There was a golden age of aviation, the building is saying, and it is perhaps possible to recapture some of that.

Foster himself is on record as saying he wanted to reclaim the simplicity and clarity of early aerodromes. He will talk about how his roof design functions as a reverse aerofoil, where winds hold it down rather than lifting it up. He is, however, silent on the imagery he adopted, but it is worth recording that the very essence of the English high-tech style as it evolved from the 1960s onwards, later becoming a global movement, was its 'back to the future' character, revisiting the previously neglected mechanistic imagery of the late 19th and early 20th centuries and deriving its expression and ornament from a love of the connection of finely engineered components. The three high priests of this movement in Britain – Foster, Richard Rogers and Nicholas Grimshaw – have all designed and built international airports that are assembled from precision-made pieces in this way.

Foster's American Air Force Museum at Duxford, near Cambridge, for instance, embodies multivalent imagery, all to do with planes. It can be read as – indeed is – a kind of concrete blister hangar, so is appropriate for the decommissioned military aircraft it contains. The building was set out, for instance, around the colossal dimensions of a Boeing B52 Stratofortress. It can also be read as a giant aircraft cockpit: the glazed joint where the superstructure meets the ground curving up around it suggests that the top can be slid open. Or it can be a jet engine nacelle (enclosure) or a segment of fuselage: service doors to either side of the building are reminiscent, depending on one's point of view, of the reverse-thrust openings in commercial jet engines or of the pressurized cabin doors of airliners. So not all the imagery of high-tech has to be nostalgic, though nor does it have to be quite this literal. An American contrast to Foster's Duxford might be Frank Gehry's 1984 Aerospace Hall at the California Science Center in Los Angeles. A fighter jet – a Lockheed F-104 Starfighter – is pinned to the outside like a brooch, and the entire building in its form and industrial materials picks up on the jagged dynamism of that image, but without making direct reference to it.

Nicholas Grimshaw (b.1939), to take another prime example, seems primarily fascinated by the design of today's aircraft. He has designed covered external staircases in the form of jet engine nacelles at his large 1990s expansion project

All pictures The American Air Force Museum at Duxford by Foster and Partners, 1997. It is a hangar and also a cockpit as well as an engine nacelle.

All pictures Frank Gehry captures
the dynamics of flight in his
Aerospace Hall at Los Angeles's
California Science Center, 1984.
A Starfighter sits on the front of
the building.

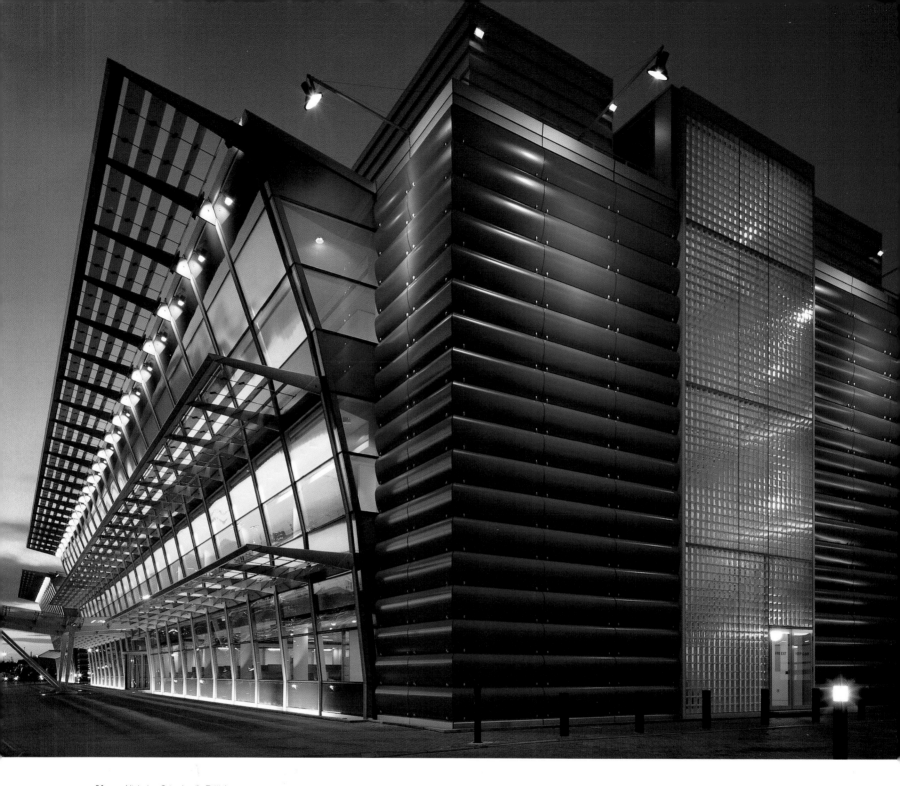

Above Nicholas Grimshaw's British
Airways Combined Operations Centre,
Heathrow airport, London, 1990-93:
the curved facade and ribbed sides
reduce its radar reflection. This is
where BA crews arrive and depart.

Opposite The predecessor of
Grimshaw's winged form: external view
of Eero Saarinen's TWA terminal,
1956–62.

for Manchester airport, although he is dissatisfied with the way the project was handled and resists its publication. His terminal expansion project at Heathrow airport, Pier 4a (1989–93), overtly refers to plane fuselages pierced with portholes, while the purpose-designed light fittings evoke aerofoils. At the same airport, Grimshaw's British Airways Combined Operations Centre (1990–93) – essentially the home base for all operational BA staff – takes a still more direct cue from aviation practice. Not only does its sharply curving façade with sunshading louvres recall the trailing-edge flap arrangements of airliners, but there is a good practical reason for this: the building had to be as near radar-invisible as possible. It is a stealth building. For his Zurich Flughafenkopf (airport head) expansion project, Grimshaw gets back to basics and adopts a winged form as the great, all-encompassing roof of the building. This brings us to another strand in the story of airport imagery: the abstract symbolism of flight.

Here we must return to America and the fountainhead of all such airport buildings, Eero Saarinen (1910–61). As Frank Gehry remarks in the introduction to this book, Saarinen reinvented the airport terminal typology at the end of the 1950s and made it all look effortless. The two great airport buildings he designed at the end of his relatively short life – the TWA terminal at Kennedy International airport, New York (1956–62), and Dulles International airport (1958–63) for Washington, D.C., in Chantilly, Virginia – explore different metaphors. The former is avian in the sense of bird-like: the latter is more of an expression of the uplift of flight through the ordering device of a great aerofoil roof.

Above Eero Saarinen (right) and colleagues construct a model of the TWA terminal.

Opposite and below The concrete shell domes of Lambert airport, St Louis, 1956. A big influence on Saarinen, by Hellmuth, Yamasaki and Leinweber.

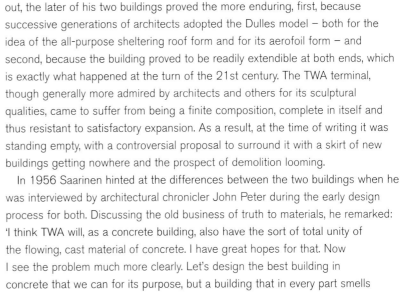

In a sense Saarinen was hedging his bets and trying it both ways. As it turned out, the later of his two buildings proved the more enduring, first, because successive generations of architects adopted the Dulles model – both for the idea of the all-purpose sheltering roof form and for its aerofoil form – and second, because the building proved to be readily extendible at both ends, which is exactly what happened at the turn of the 21st century. The TWA terminal, though generally more admired by architects and others for its sculptural qualities, came to suffer from being a finite composition, complete in itself and thus resistant to satisfactory expansion. As a result, at the time of writing it was standing empty, with a controversial proposal to surround it with a skirt of new buildings getting nowhere and the prospect of demolition looming.

In 1956 Saarinen hinted at the differences between the two buildings when he was interviewed by architectural chronicler John Peter during the early design process for both. Discussing the old business of truth to materials, he remarked: 'I think TWA will, as a concrete building, also have the sort of total unity of the flowing, cast material of concrete. I have great hopes for that. Now I see the problem much more clearly. Let's design the best building in concrete that we can for its purpose, but a building that in every part smells concrete … Very strongly I feel that a building has to be all one thing – a sense of unity in philosophy, a sense of unity in form, a sense of unity with its purpose. A building should be just one thing.'

That is the strength and the weakness of the TWA terminal, for no successful airport building, if it is to adapt and survive, should be just one thing. Saarinen had been influenced by the designs for the Sydney Opera House, for which he was a judge and for which he had that same year selected the Danish architect Jørn Utzon. He had certainly seen the shell-domes of the new Lambert airport, St Louis, Missouri. Brasilia was being planned at the time, with extraordinary organic cast-concrete buildings by Oscar Niemeyer. He refers approvingly to Frank Lloyd Wright's late masterpiece, then being built – the curvilinear, all-concrete Guggenheim Museum in New York. Taking all these influences and choosing the notion of outspread wings as his metaphor, the TWA terminal came into being as a somewhat self-indulgent exercise in the plastic arts: a wonderful advertisement for the airline but limited to a specific set of air-travel projections that would rapidly be exceeded.

When the Dulles commission came in a couple of years after the TWA one, Saarinen was already thinking differently. In the same interview with John Peter he talks in an entirely different language – the language of pragmatism rather than of sculpture. The airport professionals have clearly got to him. Asked about the importance of function, he replies: 'Well, I've gotten terribly interested in that just lately. One has a feeling that everybody has forgotten about it. That it's not the fashion anymore. But that's what we're working on … in the new international airport for Washington. Just how should an airport terminal function? What is the best method? What really happens in a terminal? What do people really do? How do they move around in a terminal and what takes time in a terminal? All these problems are fascinating and we're right in the middle of a real analysis of the problem.'

Saarinen did not study sculptural precedents for Dulles. He studied the circulation patterns of existing airports and then scaled them up to the size of terminal he was planning. He operated, in short, much as an airport architect of today operates. What are the problems? Where are the pinch points? And, as we already discussed, he looked also to an entirely different and older architecture. 'The ideal that we have,' he said, 'is really Grand Central Railroad Terminal … it is still working substantially the way it was planned and is maintaining well.'

A sea-change appears to have come over Saarinen, and it was for the good. Nor did it have an adverse affect on his architecture. Perhaps the pagoda-like Dulles control tower is a bit too tricksy for some tastes, but the bold, upswept curve of the terminal roof, supported on great raking piers, should still be any airport architect's first point of reference today. Saarinen had got to grips with the airport form, had absorbed all the complex technical issues (as one might hope from a former colleague of the famously analytical Charles Eames) and had rapidly generated a wholly appropriate abstract form for the central passenger terminal of his nation's capital. It was Grand Central station in function, perhaps, but far from that stately classical pile in appearance. It was – and is – an up-up-and-away, come-fly-with-me building, and it marks the moment when the airport began to mature as a building type.

Left Saarinen's Washington Dulles airport. The jet age spawned an aeronautical icon.

Opposite The image of soaring from earth to sky is clearly achieved on a very practical plan.

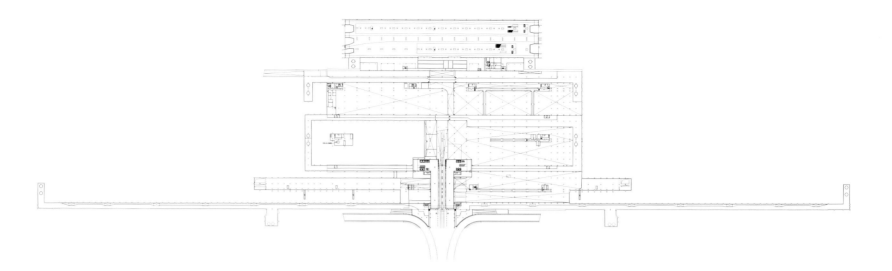

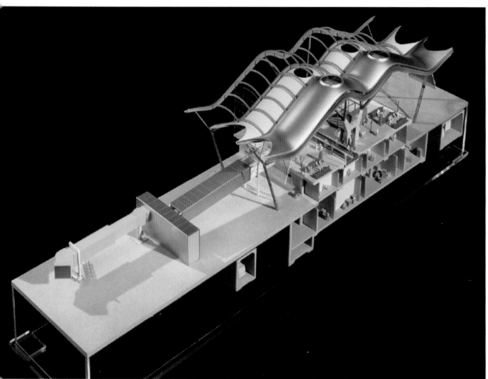

This page The latest incarnation
of Madrid's Barajas airport by the
Richard Rogers Partnership is
based on a gull-wing roof section
(1997–2005).

Opposite The outspread wings
of Pointe à Pitre Guadaloupe airport
by Paul Andreu of Aeroports de
Paris (1996) (above and below) and
roof plan (middle).

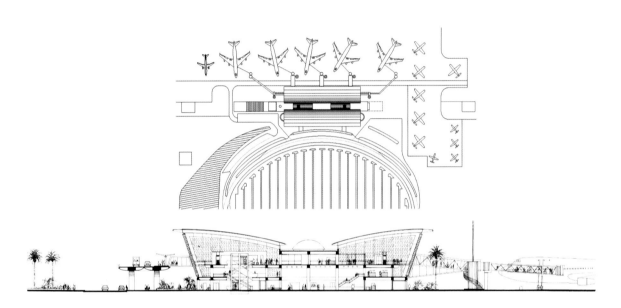

Had Saarinen not died aged only 51 in 1961, it is likely that he would have gone on to develop his ideas in a series of airport buildings. As it is, the twin metaphors – one organic, one mechanistic – of his two great airport projects provide a fertile field of reference for everyone else. Richard Rogers's new terminal at Barajas airport, Madrid, or his Terminal 5 at Heathrow, London; Renzo Piano's Kansai, Japan, with its long, long aerofoil roof; Grimshaw's Flughafenkopf in Zurich; Skidmore, Owings and Merrill's (SOM's) San Francisco; Aviaplan's Oslo Gardermoen; Paul Andreu's Pointe à Pitre International in Guadeloupe; von Gerkan and Marg's proposed new Berlin-Brandenburg – all these and many more owe a debt to Saarinen. Usually the debt is indirect, but sometimes it is overt, as with the new Terminal 1 at JFK, New York, by William Nicholas Bodouva and Associates, who try to reproduce in large-span steel trusses something of the form of the original concrete TWA terminal. A dangerous thing to attempt, but

here largely successful because the scale and materials are so very different, and this is, in addition, a matter of reference rather than pastiche. Such is the pervasive influence of Saarinen that it is even possible to claim that implacably non-Saarinen airport buildings are equally influenced by him, precisely because they react against his aesthetic approach.

No survey of the prevalence of avian or aeronautical imagery in airport buildings would be complete without a look at two key buildings by architect and engineer Santiago Calatrava (b.1951). One is the railway station for the Saint-Exupery airport at Lyons-Satolas, France (1989–94). This effortlessly upstages the airport itself. The great, curved lantern, with its feather-like steel slats above the organically shaped, part-sunken concrete concourse, is clearly enough like a bird – a somewhat sinister, vulture-like bird – poised for flight. The linking of airports with rail terminals will be considered in Chapter 6, but here it is enough

This page Named after the aviator-novelist hero, the Saint-Exupery airport at Lyons-Satolas, France, is upstaged by its railway station. Designed by Santiago Calatrava of Calatrava Vals, 1989–94, it is in characteristic avian mode.

Opposite Bilbao Sondica airport by Calatrava Vals. Is it a bird, a plane, or a whale?

This page Throughout the Sondica complex, Calatrava deploys his imagery. A fusion of bone-and-sinew, the organic and the mechanistic.

Opposite There is an unmistakable sense of dynamism in Sondica's main concourse, while the imagery outside is one of a building poised for flight.

to note that the connecting buildings between the two modes of transport can yield such fine architectures of their own – such as the deceptively simple delta-wing of the link building between Copenhagen airport's new Terminal 3 and the railway station, both by Vilhelm Lauritzen AS.

Calatrava's other contribution to the architecture of flight at the close of the 20th century was Bilbao's Sondica airport. This industrial city in northern Spain put itself on the world's cultural-tourism map with the opening of Frank Gehry's Guggenheim Museum there. As part of a concerted upgrading of the city's transport facilities it was necessary to provide a point of entry at Sondica airport that was worthy of the architectural treat in store. Calatrava's firm, Calatrava Vals, supplied the necessary uplifting imagery: there is the characteristic avian motif, with the roof of the central terminal building resembling a bird with its wings folded back. But things are a little more complex than this. There is also a curious

prow to the building that is not so much like a beak as the snout of a whale,
complete with baleen plates. A mixed metaphor, presumably referring to Bilbao's
maritime history.

How far should architects go? How literal should they be in indicating that a
building will transport people from ground to air? Some architects see airports
as being wholly things of air. Others regard planes as being more properly the
things of air, and the buildings as necessarily earthbound, so why pretend? One
answer is to combine the two elements. At Greater Buffalo airport, which serves
the Niagara Frontier region, the composition of architects Kohn Pederson Fox
(KPF) once more culminates in a wall that takes the familiar Dulles-derived form
of a wing in flight. However, this is not the end of the story, because KPF had
stopped to think about the ground–air relationship. 'This relationship can be
thought of as heavy versus light, static versus dynamic or solid versus void,' they
explain. 'Our design attempts to give physical representation to these basic
dualities.' Buffalo is therefore not a one-liner design: landside is solid, of curving
concrete, while the airside is light and glassy. The passenger is made fully aware
of the transition from point to point.

Elsewhere, the image is simply that, a marker. The be-stilted flying saucer of
William Pereira's 1960 Theme Building (obviously a working title that never got
changed) at Los Angeles International is a restaurant and observation deck, but
expressed in a separate structure that is essentially a great big sign. Similarly
the rocket-capsule form atop the transport interchange of Seoul's mighty
Incheon airport (interchange by Britain's Terry Farrell, main airport by America's
Fentress Bradburn) does have a function – as a wind-channelling device to aid

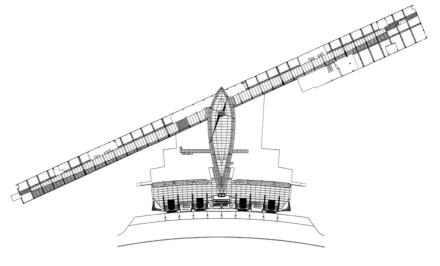

Above Trailing-edge architecture: the projected design of Xian Xianyang International airport, China, by Llewelyn-Davies.

Below At the Incheon interchange, one is brought back to the future of *The Shape of Things to Come.*

Opposite Incheon airport transport interchange by Terry Farrell and Partners. This is not a landed spacecraft, but an aid to natural ventilation in the building below.

natural ventilation of the building below – but is really there principally as a signifier of the world of futuristic transport.

The imagery of flight in all its manifestations is an example of this particular building type growing up. If the earliest commercial airports looked to stations, seaports and such other buildings for their references – and if many others in the middle years of the 20th century chose to adopt something of the vernacular architecture of their region in an attempt to make the new type fit in with its surroundings – the emergence of the buildings that take their stylistic and organizational cue from the business of flight itself showed that the type was starting to establish its own character. A railway station is free to look like a railway station and that includes the grand, even fantastical, hotels that were attached to many such stations in the late 19th and early 20th centuries. But while airports could and did learn from the hard-learned people-processing characteristics of railway stations, they did not have to share their aesthetic. As soon as the architecture itself began to take flight, it was clear that the full potential of the airport building and the increasingly independent nature of the airport as an urban organism were starting to be unlocked.

chapter five

Another war was over, and this time the resulting aviation infrastructure was in place across the northern hemisphere, rather than being confined mainly to Europe as it had been after World War One. Again, the conflict had resulted in accelerated technological development in aircraft – in speed, in size and now in propulsion systems as well. Following early research in the 1930s, the closing stages of the war had seen the introduction of the first operational jet-engined fighters, the 845kph (525mph) Messerschmitt 262 and its British rival, the Gloster Meteor. America was close behind with the Lockheed P80. In 1949 the first jet airliner, the timelessly beautiful, four-engined De Havilland Comet, would begin its test flights.

In 1952 the Comet entered commercial service on the London-Johannesburg run and later to India. Serious structural defects – three of the pressurized, square-windowed planes broke up in midair – grounded the fleet in 1954. A radical redesign delayed its transatlantic introduction until 1958, by which time the world-beating Boeing 707, carrying twice as many passengers as the Comet, was ready to roll alongside its great rival, the Douglas DC–8. Both were brought into being at the behest of one of the most influential figures in commercial aviation, Juan Trippe (1899–1981), who had founded Pan American Airways in 1927 and who had had much to do with the development of the airport as a building type as he expanded his route network. But Trippe found that the USA and Britain were not the only shows in town. During this mid-1950s jet-age interregnum, the Soviet Union mischievously flew its prototype jetliner, the Tupolev Tu-104a, unexpectedly into London's new airport at Heathrow in March 1956. It was a wholly successful publicity coup, and the bomber-derived plane started service on internal Soviet routes in the autumn of that year.

Even before the arrival of the jets, with all that meant for airports, however, the heavy, propeller-driven bombers of World War Two had left their legacy of long concrete runways and were to adapt readily to civilian use. Surplus Avro Lancaster bombers, converted and renamed Lancastrians, were cheap and relatively fast, and flew as far as South America. Boeing inflated the B–29 Super Fortress into the extraordinarily bulbous, very comfortable but chronically uneconomical, double-deck Stratocruiser. The Douglas C–54 Skymaster wartime cargo plane developed into the successful DC–6 and DC–7 series of airliners. On the orders of Howard Hughes of TWA, the Lockheed C–69 military aircraft was stretched to become the Super Constellation, a dolphin-like plane, still regarded by many as the zenith of luxurious prop-liner design.

The ends of some lines were reached, too. Hughes's eight-engined plywood H4 Hercules flying boat, nicknamed the 'Spruce Goose' (it was, in fact, birch) was originally envisaged as a military transport craft, but it flew only once briefly in 1947, with the boss at the controls. It is still, at the time of writing, the largest heavier-than-air machine ever built. Hughes may have been a majority shareholder in TWA, but the era of the flying boat was drawing to a close and he knew it. In Britain, meanwhile, the enormous Bristol Brabazon, also with eight engines but carrying only 100 passengers, made its test flight in 1949 and was promptly and properly abandoned. Aviation was not going in that inefficient direction. The same year saw the first flight of a likelier design, the French

Chapter Five The Post-war International Airport

B.O.A.C. Comet Jetliner

Above The peak of propliner design: the Lockheed Super Constellation, designed in 1939 for military service. It became commercial in 1946.

Left Luxurious but uneconomic, the Boeing Stratocruiser was developed from a bomber.

Opposite First but flawed: the De Haviland jet-powered Comet, 1956.

Previous A Pan American jet at the International arrivals building, 1959.

Duty Free Liquor

double-deck Breguet 763 Deux Ponts. This packed 101 passengers into a more compact form than the Brabazon, flew faster and required far fewer crew. Although it entered service, this spiritual forerunner of the Airbus A380 was not a commercial success.

But the trend was obvious. Larger, faster planes – the best prop-liners of the post-war years could exceed 560kph (350mph) – carrying up to 100 passengers had arrived, along with regular and frequent transatlantic travel for the first time. The development of still faster and bigger jet-engined planes was clearly only a matter of time, as Trippe was well aware. The world was beginning to shrink. Airports suddenly had a lot of growing up to do if they were to serve the new technology and the new passenger base wanting to use it.

In 1946 Horace Knight Glidden (1901–87) published a report on the state of America's airports. The problem was becoming familiar, especially on the east coast. 'The crowded conditions existing at La Guardia Field and the Washington National airport are examples of outgrown facilities,' Glidden wrote. 'In neither case can short-sighted planning be blamed. Air transportation has simply grown faster and to larger proportions than could possibly have been anticipated. The war has set the stage for what should prove to be an even more rapid growth.'

Although Glidden devoted much of his book to the technical operation of airports, he was fully aware of the role of terminals: 'Because buildings play such an important part in creating a favourable impression of an airport, extreme care must be taken to ensure that the layout, design, and architecture are the best,' he recommended. No doubt with an eye to the European experience, he noted that catering facilities were not only desirable for the passengers but could be 'a source of worthwhile revenue'. This was nothing less than the truth, but it raises an interesting point. By 1946 America had largely closed the gap with Europe when it came to airport design. However, another gap was slowly to open up in the post-war years: the importance of retail.

Surprisingly for a nation that essentially invented the modern shopping experience, America was slow to catch on to the retail possibilities of the airport terminal and to the captive market of customers, penned in while they waited for their flights. It is all the odder when one's considers the extensive internal air network that was starting to develop in the United States, with the concomitant waiting for connections. As it turned out, it would be Europe, especially Britain, that was to seize the initiative in this area in later years, driven by the lure of tax-free goods available in the airports of numerous handily adjacent countries. But all this was some way off. In 1946 what was needed was capacity and flexibility. Glidden stressed the need to allow for future expansion. 'Almost without exception, every terminal building constructed to date has proved to be inadequate. Many have been outgrown even before their construction was finished,' he wrote.

One solution, he concluded, was the adoption of new construction techniques. He noted that 'telescoping loading gangways', which had existed in prototype form in America and Britain before the war, were still not in use though much desired. And he recommended the use of war-proven engineering techniques – particularly in bridge and shell-dome construction – to achieve large, clear-span spaces. Both his recommendations were to be adopted.

All pictures In the post-war years, aviation finally entered the mass market, with facilities to match, as shown at Albuquerque (below) and London, Gatwick (left).

Above New York's La Guardia in
1955: the airport terminal (top) and
the observation deck and field apron.

Opposite The great carousel of
individual terminals at Idlewild (later
John F. Kennedy International) airport.
The 1952 master plan, shown here
in 1971 (below), was by Wallace
K. Harrison.

Glidden's British equivalent was S.E. Veale, whose *Tomorrow's Airliners,
Airways and Airports* (1945) was a typical example of the ruminations
concerning commercial air travel at the time. Veale graphically illustrated the leap
in scale that had occurred since the inter-war years: 'Nations are already
confronted with the prospect of paying twenty million pounds for a single airport;
and are apparently less disturbed by the inevitable expenditure of this vast sum
than they were in earlier years by the need to invest twenty thousand pounds in
an airport scheme.'

Veale's summary of what was going wrong was astute, but his prognosis for
the future (elevated airports in city centres by the 1990s) was completely wrong.
He did correctly identify the need for concrete runways to take the latest
generation of heavier, faster planes. What Peter Reyner Banham was later to
describe as the 'pastoral phase' of airports was by then over, though only just.
'Even as late as 1939, it was not uncommon for considerable portions of busy
airports to be marked off as too dangerous to use,' Veale commented. Here was
where America scored, for by 1939 most of America's major airports had
adopted the multi-runway approach rather than the circular or square multi-
directional landing field that was still current in the European tradition. However,
America had not yet got to grips with the capacity problem, and on this point
Veale was at one with his transatlantic colleague.

New York's La Guardia airport had opened in 1939 at a cost of $45 million
(then the equivalent of £10 million), yet by 1941, Veale observed, there were big
queues of planes waiting to take off and land at this showpiece portal to the city
and the nation. A mere 248 daily scheduled arrivals and departures were enough
to clog it up completely. He noted: 'It was judged one of the most up-to-date
[airports] in the United States – in the world. Yet barely two years later it was
incapable of dealing with the traffic scheduled to pass through it, and work was
started on the gigantic Idlewild scheme, itself now the target of adverse criticism
though not yet completed.'

Construction had started on Idlewild, named after a local golf course and later
to become John F. Kennedy International, in April 1942. An area of 405 hectares
(1,000 acres) of marshy tidelands on Jamaica Bay, 24km (15 miles) from the
centre of Manhattan, was commandeered and a budget of $150 million was
spent – already a sum 50 per cent larger than Veale imagined as necessary for a
new airport. When Idlewild opened in July 1948 as New York International, it was
linked with the United Nations, just set up in New York, as a key contributor to
world peace. President Harry S. Truman, speaking at its inauguration, said:
'This airport can aid directly in the work of the United Nations. It will be the
front door of the United Nations. Men and women from the far corners of the
earth will land here in their search for peaceful solutions to their countries'
difficulties. Representatives of the United Nations will take off from here for
troubled areas to make peaceful, 'on-the-spot' settlements ... We favor the
greatest possible freedom in international travel and communication, because
we know that knowledge leads to understanding. There never has been and
never can be war between nations when their peoples have known and
understand each other.'

Above The first terminal at
Idlewild/JFK, by SOM, 1957.

Below Lambert St Louis airport by
Hellmuth, Yamasaki and Leinweber,
1951–6: a key terminal design.

Opposite The original 1960 Pan Am
terminal at JFK with its later two-level
roadway system and extension.

It seems that, against all the evidence of World War Two, the 1909 optimism
that had greeted Blériot's first international flight from France to Britain was still
alive and well. It is ironic that Truman was speaking against the background of a
mighty US military air show, a complete review of the aeronautical power of the
Air Force and Navy and a demonstration of how America intended to continue its
domination of the skies and so enforce the peace. But the President saw more in
the future of flight – newspapers from Europe on sale a few hours after they
were printed would be a symbol of a new era of international trade. And he was
able to show just how world-shrinking aviation was by then becoming: 'When I
was a boy it would have taken President Grover Cleveland nearly three
weeks to go Rio de Janeiro, Brazil. But I was able to fly down to Rio last year
in 18 hours of actual travel time. I am only one of many thousands of Americans
who have become acquainted with other countries because of the airplane.'

The facts were these: in Idlewild's first full year of operation, 1949, there were
18,115 plane movements involving 222,620 passengers, more than 4,653
tonnes (4,580 tons) of cargo and 1,170 tonnes (1,150 tons) of air mail. Some
50 years later the same, much-expanded airport would be handling 32 million
passengers a year, with a proportionate increase in cargo, on a site only five
times the size of the original. This pattern of growth and compaction was to be
common to all the key post-war airports. In those early days at Idlewild
passengers used a low-key temporary concrete terminal by Delano and Aldrich,
architects of the pre-war La Guardia. The long, low building with a stubby central
control tower was a throwback to 1930s thinking. By all accounts, the three
huge steel hangars alongside by Roberts and Schaefer were more interesting.

This temporary solution was provided because political arguments were raging
over the masterplan for the airport. However, these were resolved by the end of
the 1940s when the Port of New York Authority was confirmed as the operator
of the site. The unique plan that survives at Kennedy airport today dates from the
1952 design by architect Wallace K. Harrison (1895–1981) of Harrison and
Abramovitz, a firm that was also, by coincidence, much involved with the United
Nations building in New York and would later design the headquarters of the CIA.
Harrison proposed not a single-terminal, state-sponsored solution, but a cluster
of free-enterprise terminals, operated by different airlines. This market-led
response, so different from European thinking, led to the great merry-go-round of
terminal buildings at Kennedy today. They are arranged in a doughnut formation,
with car circulation and parking in the middle, and planes radiating out round the
edge, with runways to either side. As a consequence of this dispersal of facilities,
Idlewild/JFK developed a number of different architectural aesthetics by
different hands – Tippets Abbett McCarthy Stratton with Ives Turano and Gardner
for the oval 1960 Pan American terminal (now Delta) with its great uptilted,
sheltering canopy, beneath which planes drew up à la Tempelhof; Eero Saarinen
for the organically sculptural TWA terminal; SOM for the first of all the
'permanent' terminal buildings there, the coolly modern International Arrivals and
Departures Terminal of 1957 (finally replaced in 2001 with a new, $1.4 billion
Terminal 4, also by SOM), and so on.

Idlewild learned from its forbears. All the airport designers of the day had
taken a long, hard look at the best of the 1950s airports, Lambert St Louis

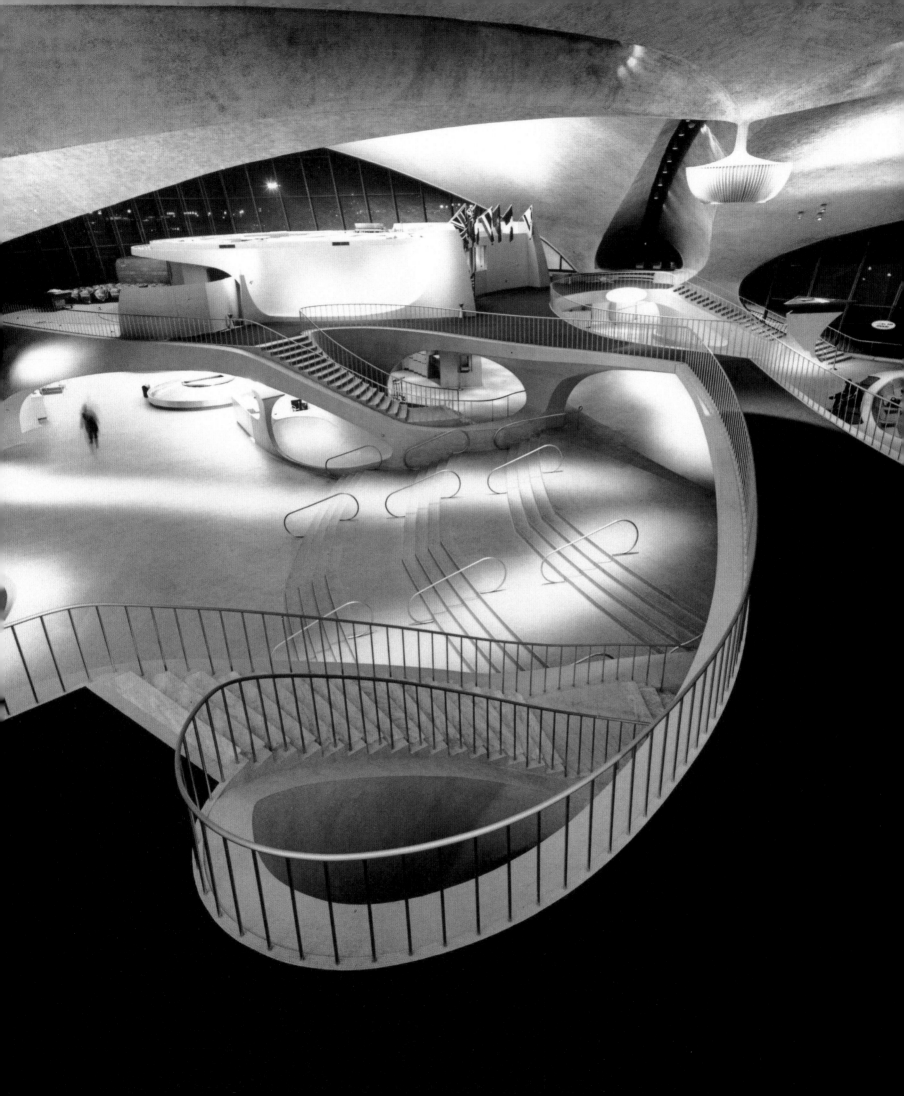

All pictures and overleaf Eero
Saarinen's TWA terminal at
Idlewild/JFK, 1956–62.

Previous The Pan Am terminal
at John F. Kennedy International,
in 1964.

International, by Hellmuth, Yamasaki and Leinweber. Replacing the original 1927 terminal, this used the concrete-shell technology that Glidden had recommended in 1946. Thin-shell concrete domes, a product of wartime technology, were at that time being seized on by progressive architects as the next big thing, a way to achieve large, clear-span spaces without the need for massive support structures. At Lambert St Louis, the young architects made full use of them. The firm was later to split up into the two practices of Minoru Yamasaki (1912–86), architect of New York's World Trade Center (1966–74), and the firm known today as Hellmuth, Obata and Kassabaum (HOK), still active in airport design. They were commissioned in 1951 and the airport was opened in 1956 to immediate acclaim. The drama of the space in the main terminal – still in existence today, though with many accretions – came from the intersection of the domes, along with a geometry that sliced the domes through to create arched overhangs on the exterior. The interior is like a fantasy of Sir John Soane, the English Georgian architect who invented such vaults in very different circumstances and different materials. Still highly impressive today, the 1956 terminal at Lambert airport, St Louis, clearly influenced other architectures, from the Sydney Opera House through to Saarinen's related TWA terminal at Idlewild. Its influence can also be seen in the calm intersecting-dome interiors of Rafael Moneo's San Pablo airport, Seville, Spain (see pages 191–3).

At London's Heathrow, which was developed at the same time as Idlewild, things began more provisionally. The area had been earmarked in 1943 for a future London airport because Croydon, set on a hill and landlocked by suburban housing, was becoming increasingly inappropriate. Heathrow seemed ideal. It was a flat district with a distinguished history of airfield operation only 19km (12 miles) west of central London, with nothing around it except some market gardens and the odd village, so there would be few protesting householders to consider. The government exercised its wartime powers to acquire 1,130 hectares (2,800 acres), and a triangle of runways was laid out; this was standard RAF practice to allow take-offs into the wind. This was later developed into a double-triangle 'star of David' configuration, with parallel main runways. On 1 January 1946 the fledgling Heathrow airport was transferred to civilian control, and the first flight out in May that year was an Avro Lancastrian of British South American Airways (BSAA), heading for Buenos Aires via Portugal, West Africa, Brazil and, finally, Argentina. It took 35 hours to get the 10 passengers and tonne of airmail there. The same day, another Lancastrian, this time owned by the British Overseas Airways Corporation (BOAC), set off for Sydney. The intercontinental, state-sponsored aspirations of the airport were thus set from the first, for these airlines, along with British European Airways (BEA), were all nationalized concerns. Airport and airlines were created as part of the same grand plan. The Lockheed Constellations of Pan Am and American Overseas Airways that were soon arriving at Heathrow from laissez-faire Idlewild represented a very different approach.

In the wet summer of 1946 the first Heathrow airport terminal was primitive by any standards. It consisted of a row of army tents on the north side of the airfield. Outside the tents were telephone kiosks and a mobile post office. Inside, however, were chintz club armchairs, a bar, a telegram service and a branch of

Above The tented terminal at Heathrow, 1948.

Below Heathrow control tower by Frederick Gibberd, 1955.

the newsagents and booksellers W.H. Smith – an early attempt at airport retail that was to become a permanent fixture. There were also some foetid chemical toilets. The tents were soon replaced by ex-military concrete prefabs, but by this time a serious master plan was being drawn up, which established the key form of Heathrow as it is today: a central cluster of terminal buildings between the main runways, reached by twin road tunnels under the northern runway. As with Idlewild, the central configuration of terminal buildings – exactly the opposite approach to that taken by pre-war omni-directional airfields, where buildings were pushed to the edges – was made possible by the adoption of permanent runways. Knowing exactly where the planes were going to land and take off allowed the designers to use much of the huge central area of the airfield for buildings. At Heathrow, the buildings were soon to swallow up three of the cross-runways.

The young architect Frederick Gibberd (1908–84) was given the task of designing the first permanent Heathrow buildings, in red-brick Scandinavian-Modern style. Construction began in 1951. The group of three buildings – control tower, passenger terminal (now Terminal 2) and the Queen's Building for restaurants, administration and spectators – opened in 1955. Much of this original architecture, although altered, is still to be seen. As at Idlewild, other terminals soon followed, all tightly overseen by the state. Heathrow was to become complex, but never nearly so unfettered as its American sister. Nor was it to enjoy anything like Idlewild's roster of top architects in the early years. Indeed, the best building at Heathrow from the 1950s is seldom seen by the public at all: it is the muscular Technical Block A – a hangar, maintenance and office complex for 4,000 staff of BOAC, from humble worker to director. The engineer Owen Williams (1890–1969) created huge, clear-span spaces using concrete cantilever techniques derived from bridge-building. A large hangar or 'pen' takes up each of the four corners; three of these were later crudely altered in order to house Boeing 747s.

In the Soviet Union, despite the early strides in jet technology, airport design under Stalin was still stuck in the pre-war era of heroic classicism, by decree. Moscow's Domodedovo airport of the early 1950s was conceived as a neoclassical palace by Stalin's favoured architect, Lev Rudnev (1885–1956), who also supervised the lighter neoclassical pavilion of Minsk airport (1950–56), working with the talented Ivan Zholtovsky (1867–1959). A parallel example is Leningrad (St Petersburg) airport, originally named Shosseynaya, now called Pulkovo. The original timber farmhouse-like terminal of 1932 gave way to larger structures in the late 1930s, which in turn were destroyed during the siege of Leningrad in 1941–4. After the war services operated from other airfields until Shosseynaya was reopened in 1948. The full-blooded classical composition of the large new airport terminal, by architect A.I. Gegello, opened in 1951. In appearance it was more like the Croydon of 1928 than the designs then being drawn up in America and Britain. The attitudinal difference between the airport building and the advanced appearance of the Tu–104 jets that were soon using it were colossal and were soon to change. A decree in 1955 by a new leader, Nikita Khrushchev, made Modernism acceptable and no Soviet – or for that matter Eastern Bloc – architect would thenceforth risk designing a building that alluded to the previous regime. However, Gegello's 1951 building has proved remarkably adaptable. Now named Pulkovo 2, it was greatly altered in the late 1980s and early 1990s to handle international flights. Restoration to something like its original appearance was, however, being proposed at the time of writing.

A very different aesthetic prevailed in Europe, although the planning of airport terminals did not necessarily advance quickly after World War Two. An excellent modern terminal of the period was built at Zurich by architects Alfred and Heinrich Oeschger between 1946 and 1953, and so slightly ahead of both Idlewild and Heathrow. This was really the 1930s enlarged, but with interesting developments. The engaged column of the control tower was moved aside from its customary central position, which was given over instead to a large, very tall, slightly wedge-shaped central public concourse overlooking the apron. This space, which widened out towards the airside and became progressively lighter, introduced an element of drama as well as providing an intuitive route through the building. However, such buildings were still predicated on the notion that passengers would walk out from the building to their ever-larger, ever-noisier planes, which perforce had to park further back from the face of the building.

Even so, this model worked quite well for quite a long time. Eventually, however, with ever-increasing passenger numbers and the arrival of even larger passenger jets parked steadily further away from the terminal, ways of getting passengers from building to plane under a form of cover other than a basic canopy became imperative. Buses came first, with Amsterdam's Schipol airport being the first to employ them. Dulles employed specially designed 'mobile lounges', which could raise their passengers on scissor-lifts to the height of the plane doors; the model adopted at other airports, including Philadelphia. It is easy to forget today, when relatively quiet turbofan jet engines are the norm, just how frighteningly noisy early jets were. This exposure to extreme noise was one of the principal factors leading to the design of the enclosed airbridge, taking the passenger directly from terminal to plane, although this method did not begin to be implemented widely until the 1960s and did not become universal at large airports until as late as the start of the 21st century.

By the late 1950s a new generation of airports was starting to emerge that engaged directly with the problem of passengers having to cover increasing distances to get to the planes. In 1948 architects Ralph Burke Associates had proposed a radial central terminal with Y-shaped piers for what became Chicago's main airport, O'Hare International. It was a pleasingly symmetrical model, with the runways adopting a pinwheel formation around the central terminal area. Modified to handle much more land and air traffic by C.F. Murphy Associates (later Murphy/Jahn), this was pretty much how it came to be built in the 1950s. O'Hare was declared completed in 1963 by none other than President John F. Kennedy and, inevitably, was overcrowded within five years.

The pier or 'finger' system was adopted elsewhere, at airports such as the greatly expanded Copenhagen (by the same architect, Vilhelm Lauritzen, who had designed its jewel-like late-1930s terminal; see pages 69–71), at London Gatwick by Yorke, Rosenberg and Mardall, and at the new Orly airport, Paris, by Henri Vicariot of Aeroports de Paris. This European triumvirate of airports, all in the International Modern style and rational rather than exuberant, marked a new

Below The neoclassical Moscow airport in Domodedovo, 1952.

Opposite below Air France flew
Constellations across the Atlantic
during the 1950s, as advertised in a
poster design which reads, 'We know
how to fly'.

This page and opposite above
Zurich's transitional terminal by Alfred
and Heinrich Oeschger, 1946–53.

maturity in the design of terminals and the gradual emergence of two key factors: the large central space and subsidiary wings, providing plenty of space for planes to pull up to.

What the new airports had was scale. It is still an uplifting experience to walk through Lauritzen's 1960s terminal at Copenhagen's Kastrup airport – Denmark's largest construction project at the time – with its sophisticated sequence of levels and calming circular rooflights. Shop units subsequently cluttered up these noble spaces, but more recently, as subsequent buildings have appeared, they have to some extent been cleared out, so returning the space to its 1960s vastness. The 160m (525ft) long building was built to accommodate the new jets, and this was controversial: Kastrup is close to the city and to residential areas, and in 1958 the noisy new Caravelle twin-engine jets of SAS and the jets of other airlines had led to howls of protest and a looming political crisis. Denmark came close to building a complete new airport on an offshore island, but by 1960 ways had been found to reduce and deflect some of the noise, so the airport remained at Kastrup. As a result, Copenhagen still has one of the most convenient and congenial airports in the world.

Where Copenhagen and Gatwick adopted the form of a rectangular main airport building with a spine of accommodation stretching out at right angles to provide aircraft docking spaces, Orly configured itself in a very modern way, familiar to us from the latest airports. The central building has low wings shooting off to either side. In a way this was a return to the successful models of early German airports and the curving wings of La Guardia, but at Orly there was a far greater difference in scale between the eight-storey centre and the two-storey extensions. Not for nothing are these spines or fingers generally known as 'piers' – the principle is exactly the same as moorings in a marina. Orly brought a new importance to the terminal type: from end to end on the airside it was 700m (2,300ft) long. The central building alone, which was 200m (660ft) long, was still significantly larger even than spacious Copenhagen. Parisian airports, particularly the later Charles de Gaulle, were to try every possible configuration of buildings, piers and satellites over the next few decades, but the Orly model proved to be an enduring one and not just in functional terms. In the nouvelle vague French cinema at the time the backdrop of the glassy, ultra-modern, ultra-chic Orly was to become familiar.

At Los Angeles International, however, a different sort of film was in the mind of architect William Pereira when he created the extraordinary Theme Building (1961), a restaurant on great, curved stilts like a Martian invader from *The War of the Worlds* (1953). Pereira's brother Hal had been art director on that movie. This was image-making on a grand scale, the imagery being of spaceships rather than of conventional flight. Nonetheless, it was described as 'the first terminal area specifically designed for the jet age'. Pereira delegated much of the design to fellow architects Paul Williams, Charles Luckman and Welton Beckett. Futurism was back.

A period of experimentation ensued as airport designers sought to find the most efficient ways of getting people and planes together. Like plants budding in spring, existing terminals sprouted piers that, in turn, sprouted smaller piers, while new terminals tried out radial and linear systems. By 1967, for instance,

Above The new Orly airport, Paris, in 1971, by Henri Vicariot marked the emergence of the modern linear terminal.

Opposite Chicago O'Hare airport was destined to become one of the world's busiest, and developed surprisingly late.

Amsterdam's Schipol had arrived at a rather beautiful symmetrical ground plan that combined the Orly lateral wings (only cranked at the ends) with the Gatwick and Copenhagen type of projecting pier, which then bifurcated into two more piers. The result, in plan, was the perfect ideogram of an aircraft, complete with wings and tail, or of a standing human figure. It was not dissimilar to the layout that Norman Foster was to adopt at the end of the century with Hong Kong's Chek Lap Kok. And, of course, by the 1960s it was necessary (as had already happened in later phases of Gatwick) to have moving walkways. The distances travelled within the terminal buildings were becoming extreme. Which was why the next generation of airports was to play with the idea of the circular or hexagonal terminal, sometimes with satellite piers, so that aircraft could draw up all round.

The in-the-round system was successfully tried at Toronto (1964), Cologne-Bonn (1970), the new Berlin Tegel (1970) by von Gerkan, Marg and Nickels (Meinhard von Gerkan and Volwin Marg became famous airport designers) and most single-mindedly at Charles de Gaulle Terminal 1 by the great Paul Andreu of Aeroports de Paris. There, the diagram is perfect: the circular mother-planet is surrounded by its many moons, to which it is connected by moving walkways beneath the aprons. That was the culmination of a particular line of inquiry, but it was by no means the end of the story.

With so many ideas floating about, what might the airport become? Peter Reyner Banham, the perceptive and lateral-thinking architecture and design critic, was able to describe the entire history of airports and airliners perfectly adequately in a few hundred words in Britain's *Architectural Review* of October 1962. The magazine considered the rapid sprawl of international airports in a special section with the umbrella title 'The Landscape of Hysteria', a phrase taken from Stephen Spender's poem, 'The Landscape near an Aerodrome'. However, Banham's admirably concise essay, 'The Obsolescent Airport', showed that he was no better than anyone else when it came to predicting the built consequences of the jet-based future. Banham noted that airside buildings at Idlewild 'are being crusted over with giant louvres to deflect the jet-blasts – the first harbingers of a transportation revolution that may prove as drastic as that of the Thirties'. So far, so cautious, but from this Banham drew a huge and wholly unsupported conclusion: 'In consequence, the status of practically every building on the airfield is being questioned. With the jets growing so big, it begins to look better sense to take shelter to the aircraft when they need servicing, rather than try to cram them into hangars. Whatever finally happens with super-buses or mobile lounges, there are very strong opinions in favour of shrinking the passenger buildings to a minimum, so that the one-building type that belongs unmistakably to airline operation may be doomed even before architects have learned how to design it. Certainly, the emphasis lies increasingly on the continuity of the process of transportation, rather than the monumental halting places along the way.'

Wrong on all counts. And this was written at a time when Saarinen's Dulles terminal in Washington – the first airport designed specifically for jet planes – was about to open and convincingly disprove the case. However, Banham, wily as ever, then put the counter-argument, so ensuring that he would not become a

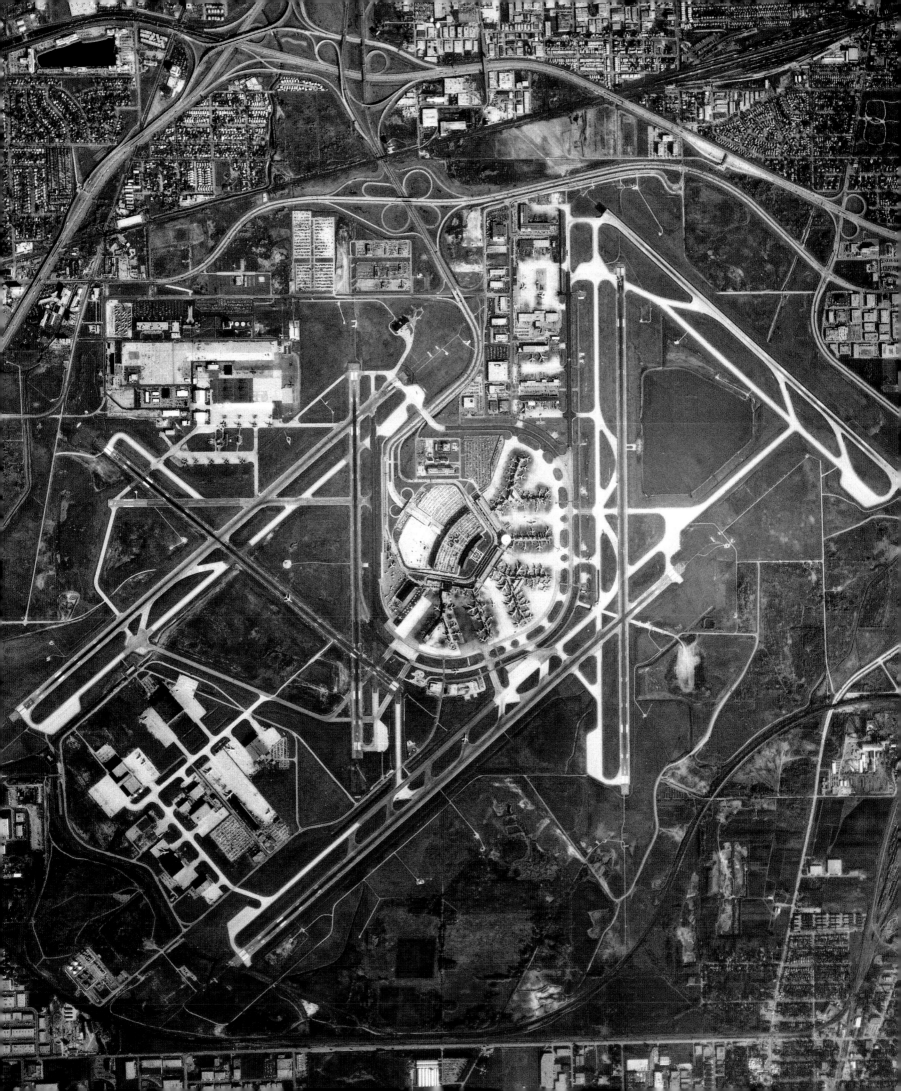

hostage to fortune: 'But will anyone let it happen? Even in the teeth of ruthless accountancy it may still be good public relations, and therefore good business, to make some concessions to the spirit that built the Euston Arch, to have some structure (even underground) where the traveller may look round and sense the excitement of being poised at the beginning of the fantastic adventure of being in New York faster than the sun can pace him, or in Sydney in 24 hours. The perennial drag of airport design behind airline operation may here have found its most massive and ultimately irreducible ball and chain – the unreformed human desire to create places for things to happen in.'

Banham thus, not untypically, has his cake and eats it, proposing a progressive, building-less airport future that he simultaneously contrives to suggest will be thwarted by the forces of ignorance, commerce (assumed to be bad) and conservatism. The Euston Arch reference was to a huge conservation battle of the day, the demolition of the triumphant, much-loved but functionally unnecessary Doric arch at London's Euston Station in the name of progress. The year 1962 also saw the continuing rise of the influential Archigram group of radical architectural theoreticians, which had been established in 1960. As it happened, all the members of Archigram had day jobs designing the replacement Euston Station, and their particular calling-card was the total rejection of formal architecture. In its place they put forward a manifesto of temporary, groovy, inflatable, modular, above all portable, structures that drew their language from planes and early spacecraft. Banham, always game for a new architectural fashion, was an eloquent supporter of Archigram, who also had to accommodate readers of a traditional magazine, which explains his Janus-like stance.

In one respect at least he was right: although the grand, formal terminal building or cluster of buildings was to remain as the centrepiece of the world's great airports – and indeed would stage a strong comeback by the turn of the 21st century – in the meantime, the temporary, the plug-in, the expedient would prevail. Many airports came eerily to resemble the Walking City or the Plug-in City proposed by Archigram in the mid-1960s, as extra buildings were rapidly constructed and linked to others by systems of tubes and moving walkways. What never happened was the withering away of the passenger building. This was not so much to do with 'the unreformed human desire to create places for things to happen in' as the simple fact that airports have always required people to be penned and processed. Check-in times were to get longer and longer, security was to get tighter and tighter, buildings had to accommodate ever-larger surges of people as planes got bigger and more routes were opened up, and hub airports had to be able to handle enormous numbers of people in transit.

When Banham was writing in 1962, however, airports were still in their naïve phase when a relatively small number of people – essentially an elite business

class – travelled from point to point with minimum hindrance. Although Banham imagined one different future – a future of extreme efficiency in people-processing – he failed to predict the massive growth in dwell-time that would have exactly the opposite effect. And this has always been and will always be the trouble with transport predictions of all kinds. Extrapolating from the present is still statistically the surest mode of prediction, but we must remember that in the 1890s futurologists were predicting that cities would be overwhelmed by the manure from massively increased horse traffic.

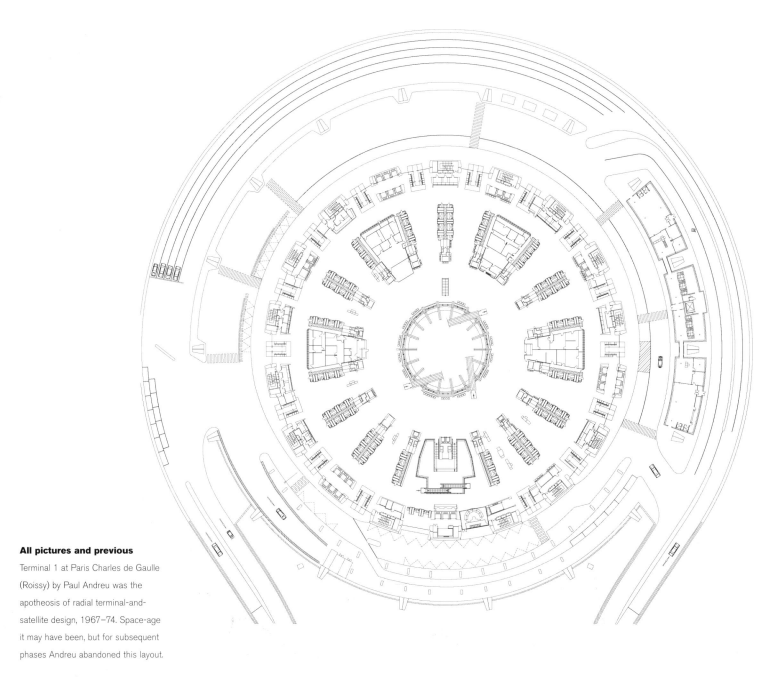

All pictures and previous

Terminal 1 at Paris Charles de Gaulle (Roissy) by Paul Andreu was the apotheosis of radial terminal-and-satellite design, 1967–74. Space-age it may have been, but for subsequent phases Andreu abandoned this layout.

chapter six

There is a huge leap, in terms of both aesthetics and scale, between an iconic building, such as the oval concrete Pan American terminal of 1960 at JFK by Tippets Abbett McCarthy Stratton, and the Martha's Vineyard passenger terminal opened in 1999 by the same firm (now abbreviated to TAMS). The former is a consciously heroic evocation of the drama of flight, taking its place in the high-class architectural menagerie that JFK was becoming at the time. The latter is an exercise in timber colonial-era contextualism. The Martha's Vineyard town of West Tisbury, Massachusetts, is plainly not New York, and equally plainly the airport sited there is a far cry from JFK. Seen from one point of view, such a place is a throwback to the early days of aviation – a small airfield, a compact cluster of semi-agricultural buildings and lots of private planes as well as scheduled services. Seen from another viewpoint, it represents the future, the necessary corollary to the giant airport-cities of today that will be discussed in the next chapter. It also reveals that there is still a great diversity in the aesthetics of airport architecture.

Chapter Six Small Can Be Beautiful

There is no reason why all airports should be made of steel and glass, and Martha's Vineyard experiments successfully with relatively traditional timber construction. The task facing TAMS was to update the existing airfield of 260 hectares (650 acres), which had evolved from a World War Two naval airbase, so that all the functional requirements of a 21st-century airport terminal would be in place without disturbing the historic landscape, with its wealthy owners of holiday cabins – many of whom, of course, use the airport.

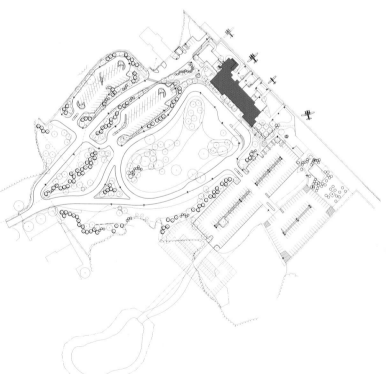

Above and opposite Martha's Vineyard terminal by TAMS (Tibbets Abott, McCarthy and Straton), 1999.

Right In an earlier incarnation, TAMS designed the Pan American terminal, Idlewild, of 1960.

Previous Frank Gehry's design for the marine interchange in Venice.

All pictures The neo-vernacular approach taken by Paul Andreu of ADP at Jakarta International, Indonesia, 1984–90.

If it were just a matter of architectural pastiche, Martha's Vineyard would be of only passing interest. Other east coast airports, such as Nantucket, ape the colonial style with more or less success – as we have seen, the local-vernacular airport is something of an American tradition. Even Paul Andreu (b.1938), airport architecture's dean of Futurism, resorted to a vernacular approach when he was designing Jakarta International in Indonesia (two phases, 1984 and 1990), with pitched-roof, overhanging-eaved departure gates conceived as summerhouses sitting in gardens. It is a somewhat deceptive image, for Jakarta is a busy airport handling the kind of passenger numbers that normally dictates a more monolithic approach to terminal design. There is nothing throwback about Jakarta's bilateral radial design, however. It is a typically elegant Andreu plan, with a tight cluster of gates rather than long fingers of piers. The external clothing is irrelevant: the design could be expressed in any style at all.

At Martha's Vineyard, however, the architecture has been designed according to sustainable principles of passive solar design and natural ventilation. A clerestory provides both stack-effect air movement and natural light (enhanced by reflective interior surfaces), while a dark slate floor was specified to absorb heat during the day and release it at night. None of this is rocket science – indeed, it is very straightforward stuff. Its importance is simply that this thinking has been applied to an airport, conventionally one of the most artificial, high energy-consuming environments imaginable, and one in the United States, where the right to air-condition is held almost as dear as the right to bear arms.

Such low-energy thinking clearly does not have to be limited to a terminal building as small as this 1,626 sq m (17,500 sq ft) example, and architects around the world are indeed taking this issue increasingly seriously. It is just that somehow all our usual judgements over what is good or bad about buildings and architecture are suspended when we enter the domain of the international airport. As a complex it is so huge, so busy, so clearly dependent on massive power consumption for everything from computer systems to the baggage-handling carousels, not to mention the scores of espresso machines in the cafes, that we become numbed by the experience. Outside, swarms of service vehicles buzz to and fro among the huge jets moving in a shimmer of tax-free kerosene exhaust, and this, too, we take for granted as just one of those things that are inevitable in air travel.

All pictures Southampton airport, England, 1993–4, by Manser Associates. An example of a low-budget airport with high aspirations, successfully deploying the image of the sheltering wing.

Of course, no legislative or tax regime is unalterable, nor are the unfettered movements of the market inviolable. It is notable that the quest for noise reduction of today's jets – which is subject to international regulation – is having the beneficial side effect of reduced fuel consumption, which is not regulated in this way. Similarly, the massive squeeze on airline profits as the industry experienced a huge economic hiccup in the early years of the 21st century intensified the drive for more efficient planes. In consequence the market value of second-hand planes – which traditionally had been high, with long lifespans expected – plummeted. Relatively young airliners, which would normally have been leased on to several different operators during their lives, were being broken up for parts and scrap. Even the budget airlines – especially the budget airlines – now prefer to buy or lease brand-new jets with more efficient avionics and engines in their quest for lower operating costs.

The world's major airports find themselves increasingly under pressure from operators to reduce their charges. One of the principal factors determining which airport a budget airline flies from and to is simply this: how high are the charges? Given that airport fees are calculated on the basis of actual operating costs and the level of demand, it follows that airports, to stay in the market, have to reduce the energy consumption of their buildings just as surely as aircraft manufacturers, to stay in the market, have to reduce the fuel consumption of their planes. Deregulation and privatization of commercial aviation in recent years have to some extent hastened this process. There are more planes flying everywhere, which is bad for the environment, but they are in cut-throat competition with each other and, mainly in Europe, with new, high-speed, international train services. This competition drives down fares, leads to demands for fuel efficiency and low airport charges, which then feed through to new generations of planes and airports designed for lower operating costs. It is not a rapid process – it takes time to develop better planes, and airports are not rebuilt overnight – but it is discernibly happening. And in this overall picture, smaller airports are starting to reassert their importance.

Small airports tend to be relatively close to the communities they serve. Some, like Martha's Vineyard and Jakarta or the new Creole-style airport at Praslin in the Seychelles, act as visual markers, indicators of vernacular architecture, to their distinctive regions. Most are more humdrum. They can never match the convenience of a city-centre railway station, but they can greatly reduce one of the great bugbears of air travel – the length of time needed to get to, and be processed through, the airport. This is of no advantage at all unless there are enough of the right sorts of flights available from the small airports, but two changes in the market in recent years have made this much more likely. The 'commuter airport' is something of a misnomer. It is not so much a matter of the same people taking the same short flight every day in the way that millions take trains, although that market obviously exists. It is more a matter of convenient business flights, usually from one financial centre to another, which expenses-paid company employees, paying relatively high fares, undertake relatively frequently. Add to that the newer market in low-cost airlines, which negotiate very low charges with – and are sometimes subsidized by – provincial airports. In recent years this has been a strong growth area.

The opening up of previously sleepy regional airports to new routes can have an electrifying effect on the local economy, in everything from holiday lets and property prices to the business in restaurants, cafes and taxis. The colonization of a swathe of southern France in the late 1990s by British second-home buyers was largely driven by the introduction of a direct route to Bergerac airport by the low-cost airline Buzz, a brand introduced by the Dutch flag carrier KLM. With just two check-in desks, Bergerac is scarcely one of the world's biggest aviation terminuses. Then Buzz was taken over by the ultra-low-cost, Dublin-based Ryanair, which threatened to axe the route. The town of Bergerac promptly came up with an annual subsidy of €550,000 ($528,000), plus a package of airport improvements, to keep the service running. It was deemed that important to the local economy. Moreover, an important local chef's school had become accustomed to sending its pupils for work experience in the restaurants of London. All this was threatened. It was a delightfully local episode, but the message has wider implications: an airport, on whatever scale, is a prime economic generator.

The incident was indicative of a new mood among airline operators – here typified by Ryanair's swashbuckling chief executive Michael O'Leary – that airports should fight for the business of airlines not vice versa. Ryanair enjoyed explosive growth in the early 2000s precisely because it chose to fly to such out-of-the-way airports on the basis of such deals, so being able to keep down its fares. In 2003, when faced with the prospect of higher charges at larger airports, O'Leary typically suggested that airports should instead pay him for bringing customers to their shops. By that time Ryanair had grown to be bigger than an old-fashioned state-monopoly airline such as Air France, so it was a view that must have struck terror into the heart of many an airport manager. In the meantime, another low-cost carrier, the tiny FlyBe, set up a route from Southampton, Hampshire, on the south coast of England, to Bergerac, so providing competition to Ryanair. The little French town suddenly found the tables turned. Having faced the prospect of no international service to Britain, it now had two. Such is the volatile nature of free-market aviation.

The downside of such bottom-line arrangements is that the true low-cost carriers will fly to the airports that are cheapest, not necessarily those that are most convenient for the cities in question. Indeed, the very fact that they are cheap will suggest that they are a long way from the action. This does not matter with rural airports that serve scattered communities, but it becomes more of an issue in urban areas. So a balance has to be struck when it comes to building the airport facilities, which must be sufficient but not lavish. Architect Norman Foster's rebuilding of Stansted airport – London's third – was rightly hailed as a triumph and a new direction in airport design, but it was, by the standards of its day, cheap. As a consequence (following some years of relative inactivity after opening, with traditional carriers shunning it in favour of London's first and second airports, Heathrow and Gatwick), it was adopted by low-cost airlines and experienced explosive growth.

However, there is cheap and cheap. Elegant, lightweight Stansted may have been economical in comparison with traditional big-budget, heavy-construction, capital-city airports, but at the real bottom of the market, money is too tight to

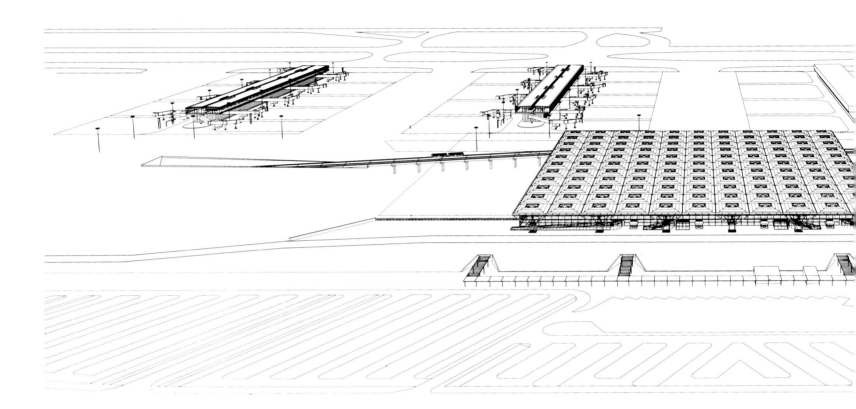

mention. To get an idea of how this thinking works, it is necessary to travel to a very different building – in which Foster's practice was tangentially involved – at what is effectively London's fourth airport, Luton. This municipally owned, privately run, traditional departure-point for cheap package-holiday charters had also come to be colonized by the new breed of low-cost carriers, notably Easyjet. When new terminal buildings were proposed for the airport by a consortium of private funders, architectural ambition had to be tempered by Easyjet's threat to go elsewhere if the place became too expensive. The result is close to being a basic functional shed, given a vague aerofoil sweep as a cosmetic styling exercise, but otherwise unremarkable. Even so, Easyjet continued fiercely to oppose the increased fees that the operating consortium tried to impose as a partial consequence of the cost of building the new terminal. So one is inclined to be dismissive of Luton, but one cannot ignore it because it embodies an important and somewhat discouraging lesson: if even such pared-down facilities are seen by the airline operators as over-lavish, there is no base architectural standard for regional airports in the low-cost era. Any shed will do. Passengers, too, appear to feel comfortable with this basic approach. When they have paid pocket money for a no-frills flight, they don't mind a no-frills airport.

Even at close to this entry-level, however, as the Manser Practice demonstrated with its low-cost Southampton regional airport of the 1990s, it is possible to produce architecture of quality. The Southampton building, with its curving roof, clerestory glazing and gently curving side wings, is a textbook

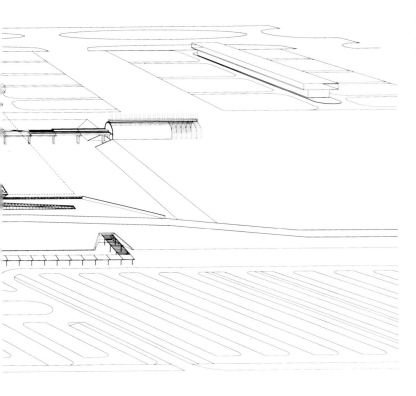

All pictures Stansted, London's third airport, by Foster and Partners, 1981–91, is a small terminal designed for expansion, as shown in the aerial perspective (top). It is notable for its highly serviced undercroft and wholly uncluttered roof (opposite and above).

exercise in making architecture out of occasionally modified standard components. When it was built it was half the price of any previous airport by the British Airports Authority (now BAA plc). Moreover, it took on an importance as a departure point for continental Europe, with travellers prepared to take a train there from London in order to take advantage of its cheaper fares and faster processing. The tendency towards ever greater size and national centralization of airports is thus counterbalanced by the customers' desire for convenience.

Stansted (1987–91, following Foster's appointment in 1981) is different because, despite its relatively low cost at the time, it was not conceived as a model for a then-unknown species of ultra-budget airport, but as a model for a new kind of international airport, and such it has become. It did not come quite from nowhere – the earlier designs for the Haj Terminal in Jeddah by SOM, for instance, provided a large, unencumbered (in that case, tensile fabric) roof in an utterly different context as early as 1977. What Foster was doing, however, was going back to the roots of the airport terminal idea, stripping away all the clutter and arriving at a building that is almost a diagram of what happens at an airport. Arrive by land – cross the concourse to the planes that can be seen on the other side – depart on a plane. The big idea of Stansted, apart from this clarity of circulation, was its lightweight modular roof of shallow domes, supported by structural steel 'trees'. The roof allows diffused daylight in and acts as a reflector for uplighters at night. The glazed perimeter was another factor in improving the quality of natural light. The roof carries no services; these are contained in an undercroft below or within the square trunks of the 'trees'. The terminal building is somewhat like a modern airliner in the sense that there is a lot happening beneath the floor about which the passenger needs to know nothing. It is also somewhat like a ship, with the undercroft as the engine room and the concourse as the main passenger deck. Foster made the Stansted basement so large that it proved possible, even as the building was under construction, to insert a mainline railway station into it.

Stansted is not a naturally ventilated building, like little Martha's Vineyard airport, but for its time it was highly energy efficient, costing half as much to run as a conventional building of its type. Its planned expansion programme, with an increasing number of satellite terminals arranged at right angles in front of the main buildings, all linked by an automated underground transit system, proceeded according to plan. So did the phased growth of the main terminal building itself. Extra modules identical to the original were simply added at both sides as needed to make what was originally a square building into an oblong one. The whole airport has a kit-of-parts feel, typical of the earlier output of the Foster practice, that has proved highly influential.

Other architects were, however, thinking along similar lines at around the same time. A prime example among smaller airports is at Stuttgart (1980–90) by von Gerkan, Marg und Partner with Karsten Brauer. There, too, are structural 'trees' supporting the lightweight roof, in that case an organic arrangement of bifurcating branches. The Stuttgart terminal is, however, arranged on a steep slope with successive interior levels. While this creates a lot of drama in the roof structure, it lacks the single-level directness of Stansted and still has some roof-level elements needing servicing, such as lighting.

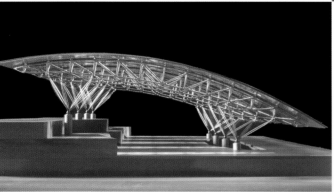

This page The clear-span structure
of Hamburg-Fühlsbuttel, 1986–93, by
von Gerkan, Marg und Partner.

Opposite above Plan of Dar El
Beida airport, Algiers, by von Gerkan,
Marg und Partner.

Opposite below Algiers under
construction. It was an unusual and
radical plan, by Meinhard von Gerkan.

Von Gerkan and Marg later refined their idea at their rebuilding of Hamburg's famous Fuhlsbüttel airport. There the structural 'trees' support long spinal trusses that in turn carry the purlins of the roof – this time unencumbered by any services and with a greater degree of natural light penetrating it. The design inspiration was less the forest canopy than the structure of a giant aircraft wing. Meinhard von Gerkan is undoubtedly one of the modern greats of airport design. His student diploma project in 1964 was a hexagonal airport design that, with relatively minor modifications, became his competition-winning entry for the new Berlin Tegel airport the following year. It was completed in 1975. Tegel, which took over from venerable Tempelhof as the then West Berlin's principal airport, is a very different concept from his practice's later airport buildings at Stuttgart and Frankfurt, or for that matter from his competition-winning Dar El Beida airport in Algiers, which has been in progress since 1981. Like Foster or Paul Andreu of Aeroports de France, von Gerkan experiments restlessly with the layout of his successive airports – the Algerian example is arranged as a semicircular main concourse that then buds into three further fan-shaped terminals, a layout he was to revisit and modify in an unbuilt design for Zurich airport in 1994.

The airports of cities such as Hamburg or Stuttgart are still relatively small compared with the vast complexes of the world's megalopolises, and this is part of their charm. Stansted, as number three in the London airports hierarchy and the furthest-flung, felt positively rural – the landscaping of the area is one of its unsung successes – on opening in 1991, although that is now becoming a distant memory as the airport and its environs develop into a sizeable township.

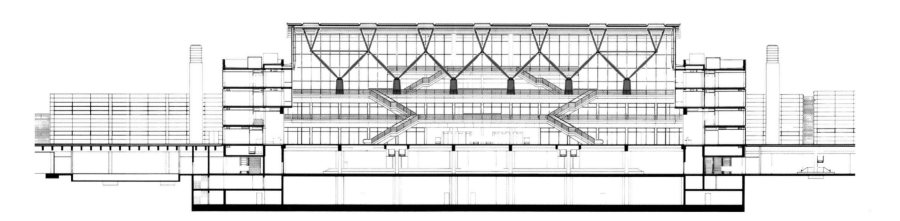

All pictures Stuttgart airport by von
Gerkan, Marg und Partner, 1980–90.
A novel structure of branching 'trees',
just predating London Stansted.

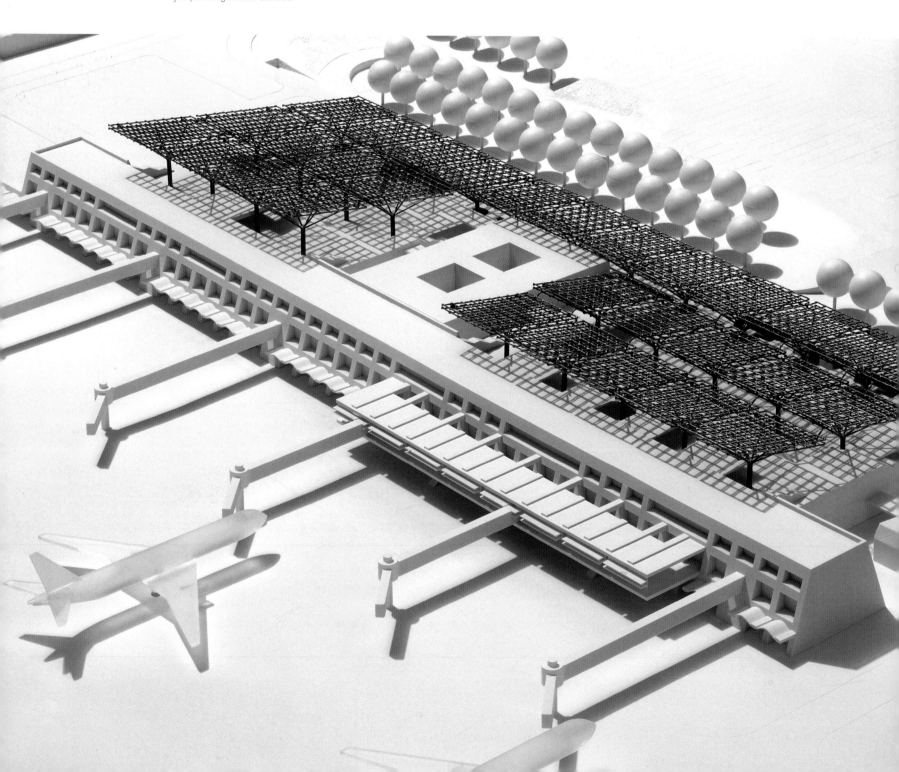

Tegel is small, since it was designed in the days of the Cold War when relatively few international visitors descended on West Berlin. The San Pablo airport, Seville (1987–92), by Rafael Moneo, a gateway to Andalucia, and Aldo Rossi's extension to Linate airport, Milan (1991–3) are interesting variants on the smaller airport theme in that they successfully attempt a different aesthetic – not high-tech, not vernacular, not classical, but an old language of solidity and allusiveness. Moneo's terminal has elements of Moorish and Roman architecture transmuted into something wholly contemporary. Taking a diametrically opposed view to the imagery-of-flight merchants, he declared: 'The perfection and lightness of flying machines have very little in common with the complex, functional mechanisms behind airports. Airports belong to the world of things built on land, and not to the sky, and are by definition places of transit.' The idea behind the great, intersecting domed vaults at San Pablo, each with its central Pantheon-like oculus, he said, was 'for the space defined by the vaults to act as a threshold to the sky'.

Rossi's companion exercise in earthbound architecture at Milan also achieves a sense of permanence and monumentality on a building type normally doomed to ephemerality. His sketches for the project show him playing around with the forms of mid-20th-century factories – masonry piers, large areas of glazing with multiple metal-framed panes, a hangar with massive columns and girders – while the passenger-loading gangways take on something of the characteristics of industrial chutes. Rossi, a manifesto-driven architect, knew what he was doing:

All Pictures Berlin Tegel by von
Gerkan, Marg und Partner, 1965–75.

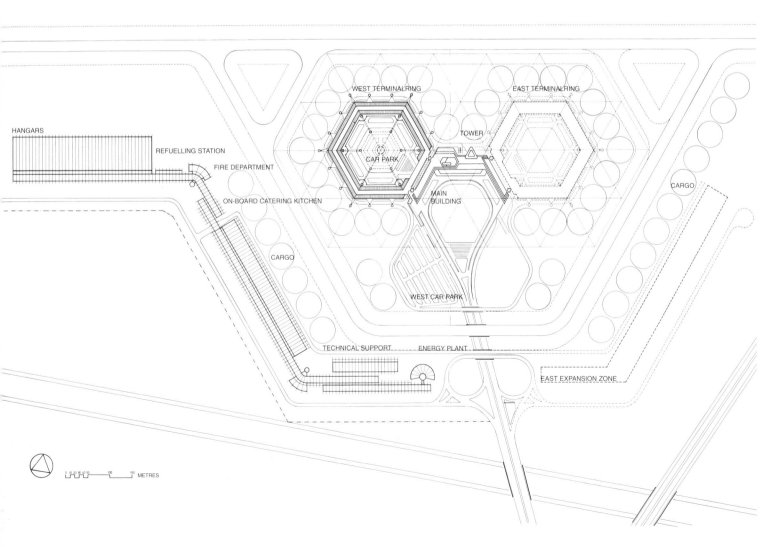

HANGARS

REFUELLING STATION

FIRE DEPARTMENT

ON-BOARD CATERING KITCHEN

CARGO

WEST TERMINALRING

EAST TERMINALRING

TOWER

CAR PARK

MAIN
BUILDING

CARGO

WEST CAR PARK

TECHNICAL SUPPORT   ENERGY PLANT

EAST EXPANSION ZONE

0 10 20 30 40 50   100   150   METRES

WEST ELEVATION

EAST ELEVATION

NORTH ELEVATION   SOUTH ELEVATION

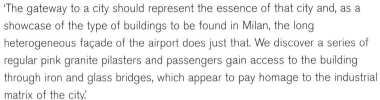

'The gateway to a city should represent the essence of that city and, as a showcase of the type of buildings to be found in Milan, the long heterogeneous façade of the airport does just that. We discover a series of regular pink granite pilasters and passengers gain access to the building through iron and glass bridges, which appear to pay homage to the industrial matrix of the city.'

So here we have airports compact enough and bold enough to express the historical identities of their cities. But what of places where there is no city? Take the grandly named Learmonth International airport, Exeter, Australia, built in 1999 by Perth-based architects Jones Coulter Young. This colourful little terminal building with its organic forms, set unexpectedly in the arid, red Cape Range landscape between the Ningaloo Reef and the Exmouth Gulf, is an anticipation of the underwater experience of swimming, as tourists do, among the exotic wildlife of the reefs. There is more. While the fit-out of the building is intended to evoke the brightly coloured, darting or floating creatures of the reef, the form of the building itself, laid out to either side of a central service spine, is inspired by the body of a whale shark, complete with external louvres for gills. Once in the terminal, passengers are like Jonah in the belly of the whale.

This charming and witty airport building – which could not be more different from most airports with 'international' in their titles – does not overplay its hand. It is nicely judged. Australia in general – a continent where flying great distances across unpopulated wastes is part of the national psyche – has an unforced joie de vivre about its airports, small or large, that can sometimes have more of the air of the pioneering airports of the 1920s and 1930s. It is easy to forget that the vast bulk of the world's airports are still relatively small, out-of-the-way places. Even a gateway to a nation, such as New Zealand's Auckland International, can

All Pictures and overleaf

Learmonth International, Exeter, Australia, by Jones Coulter Young. This structure suggests the airport as marine organism.

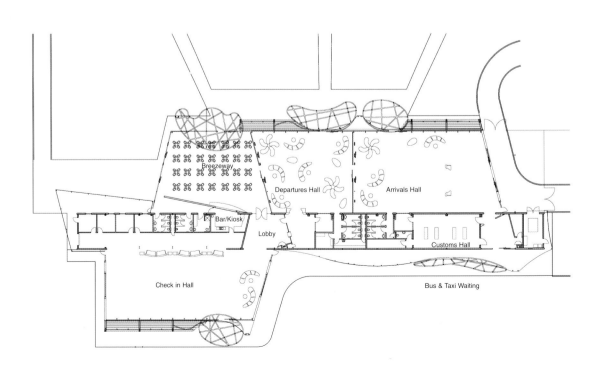

have a sense of domesticity, as the child-like, three-dimensional plans that help people find their way around make clear.

Elsewhere, cities adopt different visual markers. The fast-expanding city of Lille in northern France, for instance, with its architectural showpiece of downtown Euralille (1989–96), masterplanned by Rem Koolhaas (b.1944), is a well-connected place with a fine station on the high-speed railway. Its airport, accordingly, is a relatively modest but visually ambitious affair by Atelier Sloan with Laloux-Lebecq. It has a skewed, angular construction that, viewed across the flat fields of the region, looks more like a group of aeroplanes than a building.

All these examples are gesturalist architecture of one kind or another. This is, however, not just a matter of picking the appropriate symbolism; it is also a way of making a building seem bigger than it is. The reason for this is that it is a way of giving a city a sense of grandeur and importance – an airport is a civic gateway of the kind the Romans used to build. But there is another reason. Surrounded by wide open space as they are, terminals sometimes have to shout and wave in order visually to command their estates. Otherwise, a purely functionalist shed, hunkered down on the tarmac, risks vanishing from view altogether. It takes a steady nerve to design an airport building that is simply a nicely detailed, rectangular building, as is the case with Riegler Rewe's passenger terminal at Graz airport, Austria (1989–98). It is an interesting case because Graz had developed a tradition of austere Modernism in the 1990s, which the airport reflected perfectly, as does the projected second terminal by Pittino and Ortner.

Venice's Marco Polo airport was entirely rebuilt in 2002 to designs by Gian Paulo Mar and – with its masonry and copper and trabeated pavilions – is somewhat in the spirit of the late Aldo Rossi. This is the tourist airport in excelsis. In reaction to the cramped nature of the former buildings, the interiors of the new airport can seem almost too large, with acres of space in which to mill around. But Venice's trump card is, of course, water. The joy of the old airport was the way passengers could walk out of the main terminal and find themselves at the water's edge, where they would pick up a boat across the lagoon to the centre.

Above Auckland airport, despite being New Zealand's point of entry, has almost a village atmosphere.

Below Lille airport, France, by Atelier Sloan with Laloux-Lebecq, uses an expressive approach.

Opposite Graz, Austria, by Riegler Rewe and others, 1989–98, uses a more restrained approach.

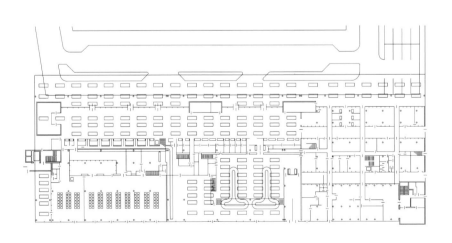

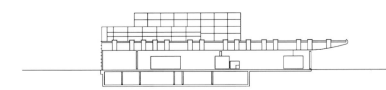

Above Frank Gehry's design for the
marine interchange at Marco Polo.

Opposite Venice Marco Polo by Gian
Paulo Mar, 2002.

The experience, one imagined, was a little like those of the maritime terminals of the flying-boat era. The distances are greater at the enlarged airport, which had to be built further away while the old terminal remained in operation, but the principle remains the same and is to be expanded. Instead of simply being a trans-shipment point, there will be a new township of hotels, offices and conference buildings by an expanded waterway, while the whole complex will link back to the new airport by a covered moving walkway. To celebrate this new gateway to Venice, the airport authority subsequently commissioned Frank Gehry (b.1929), who designed an inspired roofscape of what might be seen as jostling waves, hulls of boats, the sun sparkling off water ... the closest Gehry had come to a real airport project since as a young man he worked for William Pereira in the 1950s. Gehry's take on context is always multivalent. His roofscape is to be made of polished metal over timber, which is as much a reference to the timber-ceilinged buildings of Venice's famous naval workshops, the Arsenale, as it is to boats and planes. As a mediation point between sky, earth and water, it will certainly be unique.

This page and opposite

Shenzhen airport, China, 2001, by
Llewelyn-Davies architects.
The European terminal goes East.

It is certainly the case that a smaller airport can be more satisfying to the
architect, simply because it is a more compact form – more like a building, less
like some kind of engineering system – and so perhaps lends itself to more
traditional architectural solutions. There is a need to get a certain number of
people to and from their planes; there is a need to allow for expansion; there
must, of course, be administrative offices; and there is a need to provide a level
of facilities beyond the regulated ones of passport control, baggage handling and
customs. If nothing else, there must be a cafe and toilets. The difference
between these and the world's mega-airports is the same as the difference
between a high street shop and an out-of-town super-mall. Within the regional-
airport genre, however, there are obviously wide differences. The tiny Jyväskylä
airport, Finland (1988), by Pekka Helin and Tuomo Siitonen, for instance, handles
fewer than 250,000 passengers a year. Venice handles 6.5 million, which is
about the same number as the new Austin-Bergstrom International airport at
Austin, Texas, by Gensler architects, where a former military airbase that was
being closed down is being reused, suddenly providing Texas with the opportunity
to improve its air links, and with all the economic benefits this would bring.

In China a prime example of the genre is Shenzhen, Guangdong province,
where British architects and planners Llewelyn-Davies designed a compact and
agreeable second terminal, completed in 2001, on what might be called the
Stansted-derivative model. The lightweight canopy roof floats above transparent
walls. Shenzhen was a new airport, first opened as recently as 1991, when it
immediately became China's seventh busiest on the basis of internal flights only;
these are still the key market for China, so huge is it, despite increasing

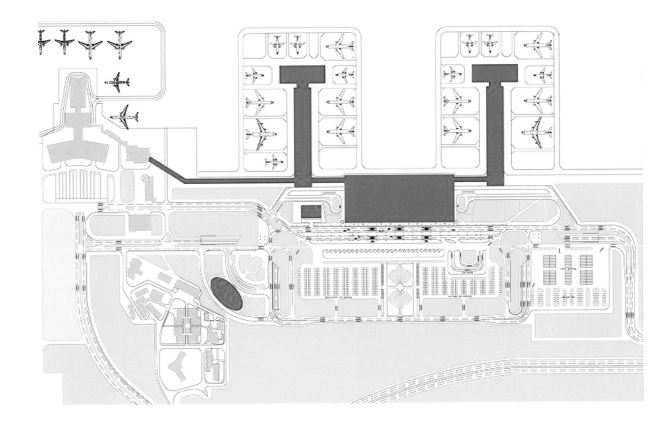

Above The simple and extendible Chongqing masterplan.

Opposite top Beihai airport, close to the Vietnamese border, as envisaged by Llewelyn-Davies. The airport is part of China's huge internal air expansion.

Opposite below Llewelyn-Davies architects with Arup: design for Chongqing Jiangbeii International, China

international traffic. As the only airport in China that combines air, road and sea transportation in a single hub, it has been growing apace – and may expand further, out into the sea. Llewelyn-Davies went on to design terminals at Chongqing in Sichuan province, Xian Xianyang in Shaanxi province and Beihai in Guangxi province, close to the Vietnamese border, as part of the gradual opening up of the Chinese market to Western expertise.

Even a national gateway airport can be small: New Zealand's Auckland, say, or Israel's Ben Gurion International airport, Tel Aviv. Despite being one of the busiest airports in the Middle East, Ben Gurion's business is as much in cargo as passengers, with most of the country's exports departing by air. Passenger numbers have also grown substantially, however, forcing Israel finally to abandon its existing airport buildings, which were the legacy of the former British Mandate in Palestine and which had been built in the late 1930s as a staging post for Imperial Airways. The new Ben Gurion terminal, opened in 2002, is a hybrid. There is a main rectangular building (by SOM with Karmi Associates and Lissar Eldar Architects), with a long, narrow link building leading out to a large, toplit rotunda from which four, and eventually five, concourses radiate, each serving eight gates (this part by Moshe Safdie and Associates and TRA). The plan is

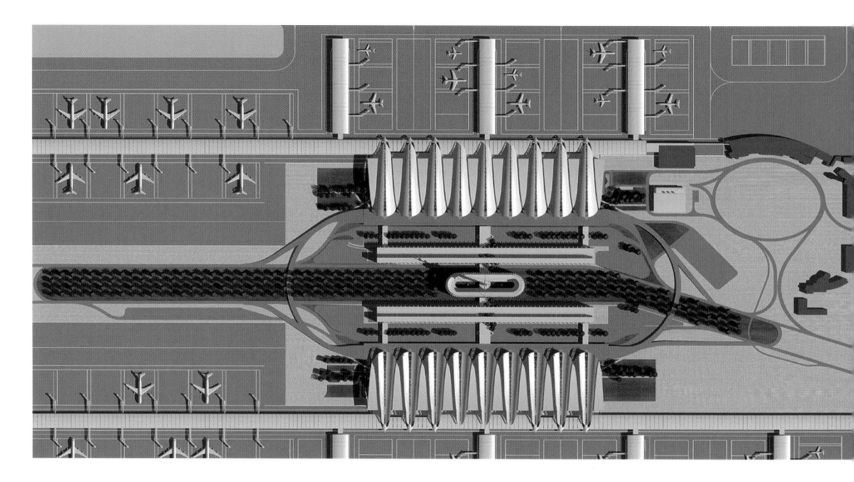

clearly much influenced by security planning – Ben Gurion is the most security-conscious airport in the world, and many passengers check in their baggage the day before their flight. The rotunda is well away from the approach roads, and the way to it is relatively narrow and easily controlled. Passengers also have to pass through a massive wall, 8m (27ft) thick. Both buildings are set in open space, readily surveyed. But it is also a compact plan, in an area of environmental sensitivity and much local housing. As the portal to a nation, it sets out to provide a feel for the natural features of the landscape. Consequently, the open aspect of the buildings has been exploited in landscape design, with terraced gardens bearing local plants providing the setting. That deep wall, faced in Jerusalem stone, has a symbolic as well as functional purpose, providing the clearest symbol of transition from earth to air, for on the airside, once all security checks have been passed, the walls open up to transparency.

It becomes increasingly important for smaller or poorer countries not to be bypassed by international trade and to be able to hold out the net of a state-of-the-art airport to catch it as it flies by. Jorge Chavez airport at Lima, Peru, one of the highest in the world, is embarking on a £80 ($120) million expansion programme by private operators Alterra Partners, a subsidiary of Bechtel. Throughout South America – which was, after all, a pioneering region for early air

This page Ben Gurion airport, Tel Aviv, Israel, 2002, is the most secure airport in the world. It is also a statement of national identity. It was designed by SOM, Karmi Associates, Lissar Eldar Architecs, Moshe Safdie and Associates and TRA.

Opposite Xian Xianyang is a bilateral terminal design where the tapering roof forms visually funnel passengers to the spines of the departure gates. Design is by Llewelyn-Davies architects.

travel – plans are being laid to upgrade the smaller airports. Brazil, still a country of few roads, scattered towns and cities with vast distances between them, has a complex network of internal flights and is building to accommodate them with a big programme, including some interesting new airport terminals at Fortaleza, Salvador, Natal and Recife. Argentina, too is building, though slowly, because of the country's economic woes. Having privatized 33 of its airports, it commissioned development masterplans for 16 of them from US airport architects Leo A. Daly. At the core of these is a plan to combine two existing Buenos Aires airports into one, Ezeiza International. The first of two new terminals has been built. Similarly South Africa – another pioneering aviation nation under colonial rule – is significantly expanding its three international airports. Cape Town's new terminal, by Harris & Harris and Nazeer Seria, opened in 2000, Johannesburg opened its new Terminal B by Associated airport Architects in 2002, and Durban is next on the list with the most ambitious expansion so far, by Aeroports de Paris.

Holiday and vacation destinations such as Ricardo Bofill's Pablo Picasso
airport at Malaga (1986–2001), a rare example of a modern full-blown
neoclassical airport, must cope with seasonal flows of passengers. Malaga had
the additional complication that it was intended to mop up some of the extra air
traffic expected to be generated by Expo 92 in Seville, and was thus seen in
terms of air traffic as a partner to Rafael Moneo's San Pablo airport in that city.
Whatever the rationale – Expo 92 was, in fact, something of a damp squib – the
upshot was that Malaga found itself with an airport that at first glance could
have come from the Soviet Union under Stalin. The terminal consists of a pair of
large, linked, pitched-roof classical buildings engineered to provide – this is a
Bofill trademark – large, uninterrupted internal spaces.

In contrast to such holiday destinations, Bofill's much larger Barcelona
terminal (originally 1988, with plans now proceeding for a new South Terminal)
had to gear up for the business traveller and tourist alike. Just like little

FINGER   EMBARKMENT DOOR   RAMP   BAGGAGE HALL
REMOTE POSITION RAMP   EQUIPMENT PICK-UP   ARRIVALS HALL

SALIDAS NACIONALES ✈ Domestic Departures

NACIONALES   ic Departures

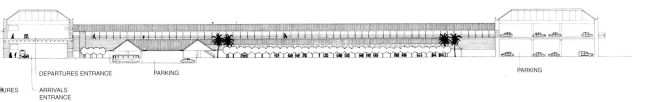

DEPARTURES ENTRANCE　　PARKING

PARKING

URES　ARRIVALS
ENTRANCE

Bergerac in southern France, mighty Barcelona found itself a destination of
choice for the low-cost airline industry in the late 1990s, and this, together with
all the full-service airlines operating there, led increasingly to overcrowding.
Bofill's terminal was originally built in 1988 in anticipation of the 1992 Olympic
Games. It served the Olympics well, but visitors kept on coming. Barcelona, one
of the most successful cases of cultural regeneration and a model to cities
around the world for just that reason, went on getting more and more desirable
to international travellers. Between 1992 and 2002 passenger numbers more
than doubled from 10 to 21 million. To put that in context, it meant that
Barcelona and Catalonia were receiving about 25 per cent more visitors by air
than each of the Scandinavian capital cities of Copenhagen, Stockholm and Oslo,
five times more than Buffalo-Niagara, and nearly as many as Philadelphia or
Munich. By any reckoning, it was not a small airport any more.

For his first Barcelona terminal, which, at 1km (1,100 yards) long, seemed
enormous at the time, Bofill downplayed the grandiose neoclassical language for

which he had become known and produced instead a composition of smoked-glass curtain walling with a saw-tooth arrangement of triangular gates projecting from the main volume of the terminal. He thus had a legible building with a clean façade, despite the usual sprouting tendrils of airbridges – free of the clutter of piers and satellites – which was fine until it was overtaken by the volume of passengers. After that, it became necessary to plan an entirely new midfield terminal, the competition for which was won by Bofill in 2001. It is planned to handle 40 million passengers by 2020 and will thus cease to be a city or regional airport and instead become a hub for the northern Mediterranean. Barcelona moves into the top division of international airports, well beyond the scale of operation considered in this chapter. It has all happened very quickly, even by airport standards.

As built, Bofill's original terminal at Barcelona – ingeniously designed with a vast hangar-like roof structure supported on just four immense columns – can still be appreciated as a single structure rather than as a complex. In this legibility – sometimes somewhat eroded by various extrusions and satellites in the form of departure gates – lies the appeal of all these smaller airports. They are essentially one-building designs – what you see is what you get. They can be read from landside to airside, and they are comprehensible places in much the same way that a well-designed regional railway station is a comprehensible, even congenial, place. Like the better railway stations, they can be places to visit for a beer or a meal or for a look around the shops, without this seeming a perverse rejection of the traditional city. With the airline industry shaking itself up thoroughly and redefining what it wants to do and who it wants to serve, it is certain that such smaller airports will play a steadily increasing role, which will restore some of the pleasure that had been leaching out of air travel around the turn of the new century.

All pictures Ricardo Bofill's Barcelona airport of 1988 signalled that city's resurgence and renewal.

chapter seven

Chapter Seven   Cities of Flight

Consider the infrastructure that was needed at our first aerodrome of 1904, Orville and Wilbur Wright's proving-ground at Huffman Prairie: a tussocky field of 34 hectares (84 acres), a hut or two – doubling as agricultural barns – to store the dismantled planes and act as workshops, and a minimum of specialist equipment out on the ground, such as a wooden launch rail and a weight-operated launching derrick. The planes themselves – the Wright Flyers – were necessarily small and fragile affairs. Once developed into a production version, they could carry one passenger or a small cargo (a bolt of silk was the first delivery) at around 64kph (40mph). Huffman Prairie had a further refinement: it was close to both a main road and an electric tramway with a convenient depot halt, Simms Station. The Wrights used to commute to the field from their bicycle shop in Dayton, Ohio.

Now consider an international airport hub a century later, of which a prime example is Denver International airport, Colorado (1989–95). It is by no means the world's most intensively used – in fact it is tenth busiest overall, and sixth busiest in the United States – but it is very large. It covers an area of 53 sq miles (137 sq km), which is twice the size of Manhattan and more than 400 times the size of Huffman Prairie. It has six runways, the longest of which extends nearly 5km (3 miles), and none of which intersect, so allowing multiple simultaneous take-offs and landings. It has a single main terminal building – Jeppesen Terminal, named for Elrey B. Jeppesen, an aeronautical pioneer and businessman whose aviation charts are at every pilot's elbow. The Jeppesen Terminal contains 139,350 sq m (1.5 million sq ft) of space, but this is not all. Three further concourses are spaced out in front of it and linked to it by an automated underground transit system. The total area of public concourse adds up to more than 557,400 sq m (6 million sq ft). The area contained within passenger buildings only at Denver thus pretty well amounts to two Huffman Prairies side by side.

So Denver International is an awesome place. It is, moreover, designed to more than double in size, both in terminal capacity and in numbers of runways. As the first new airport in the United States for 20 years – since Dallas/Fort Worth in the early 1970s – its present phase cost $3.3 billion and shows a clear determination to be future-proofed. Land has been reserved to allow for an eventual 13 runways up to 8km (5 miles) long, to give a final capacity of 100 million passengers a year. The planes it serves are, of course, gigantic compared to anything in the Wrights' experience, although they are not particularly fast, cruising at much the same speeds as the first jet liners of the 1950s. High speed, apart from the glorious 30-year supersonic anomaly of Concorde, is reserved for the military. Although the size of the plane, as we have seen, has a significant impact on the design of airports and their terminals, the key factor is numbers. Particularly in the American airline-determined hub system, where flocks of planes tend to arrive in a short period of time in order to allow passengers to change flights, it is the processing of the numbers that determines the layout. Hence Denver's extraodinarily generous runway and passenger concourse configuration.

The downside of this sprawling approach is that it can take a very long time to taxi from runway to terminal or vice versa. Despite its scale and modernity,

All pictures Denver International by Fentress Bradburn, 1989–95. The design includes the famous tented roof (opposite above) and a land-hungry runway layout (below) covering 53 sq miles (137 sq km).

Previous Athens-Sparta Eleftherios Venizelos airport, 2001.

All pictures The Haj terminal, Jeddah, (1977–92) provides shelter for pilgrims bound for Mecca (below). It is the tensile-fabric precursor to Denver (opposite).

Denver International lacks one thing that Huffman Prairie had a century ago: a rail service. It is accessed by road. While this configuration might work well in Colorado, where the airport serves a region as much as a city and is, in addition, a prime connecting point for people who never leave the airport at all, it has been found to be a major omission in most other city-centric, world-class airports. The experience of getting to and from New York's JFK along choked highways, including toll bridges, for instance, became so appalling by the end of the century that America finally learned once more from the European experience (and from the successful precedents of nearby Philadelphia and far-flung Atlanta) and in 2004 opened a rail line out to the airport.

As soon as an airport becomes twice the size of Manhattan, with buildings to match, it is tempting to state that these complexes are cities in themselves – cities of flight. Well, some are and some are not. The vastness of Denver, for instance, is mostly prairie given over to that remarkably land-hungry runway layout. At Munich, 70 per cent of the area of the airport, despite its compactness at 1,100 hectares (2,718 acres), is defined as 'green areas'. Imagine a Manhattan where Central Park, already huge, takes up 70 per cent of the city area. Even so, the interiors of terminal buildings certainly have an urban, speciality-shopping feel to them. In the Denver terminals in 2003 there were 50 cafes and restaurants and 70 shops of various kinds, including, as a historical note, several outlets of the same W.H. Smith newsagents that could have been found at the tented village of Heathrow in 1948. Tents even made a return of sorts, in the form of Denver's famously dramatic 'Great Hall' main concourse designed by Fentress and Bradburn, the white peaks of its tensile fabric roof recalling SOM's pioneering Haj Terminal in Jeddah as well as referring to the distant snow-capped peaks of the Rocky Mountains.

This page Atlanta Hartsfield and its
echelon of terminals. It is a very
influential model dating from 1966.
It is the world's busiest airport by
some calculations.

For all its statistical interest, Denver is not quite a typical mega-airport. Such relatively new hubs do not have the feel of the older airports, which developed over many years on tighter sites in a piecemeal way as real cities do. I defy anybody to find much in the way of city life – apart from the usual mix of gift shops and eateries – at a typical American hub, such as Cincinnati. Denver, meanwhile, situated so high in a mountainous region, is prone to a problem with which the Wrights were very familiar – being closed in bad weather. Winter snowfall frequently shuts Denver down, which – given its importance as a strategic part of the US air network – can lead to knock-on problems across the nation. In a funny way, and against the odds, Denver is indeed the linear successor to Huffman Prairie as a pastoral airport.

According to the figures produced by the Airports Council International, Heathrow in the United Kingdom was the world's third busiest airport in 2002, handling 63.3 million passengers. This was some years before Terminal 5 opened – proof that a relatively compact national airport with what must be regarded as the minimum of runways can somehow be made, by means of precision air-traffic control, to handle the traffic. The 'footprint' of Heathrow compared to Denver is tiny: at 1,200 hectares (3,000 acres) it is considerably less than a tenth of the size. Chicago's O'Hare airport came second, processing 66.5 million passengers in the same year, and it has many of the same congestion problems as Heathrow. Both of these were eclipsed by one of the world's more unglamorous airports, Atlanta Hartsfield, which, as a southern hub in the United States, topped the bill with 77 million passengers in 2002. It was the most delay-prone airport in the United States.

Hartsfield – another surprisingly compact footprint, at 1,518 hectares (3,750 acres) – is a phenomenon. It is planning to invest $5.4 billion expanding itself to handle an estimated 121 million passengers by 2015, 57 per cent of whom will be passengers connecting to flights going elsewhere. That is the equivalent of the entire population of the British Isles, just changing planes each year at a single airport, and it is all mostly down to one airline, Delta, whose primary hub this is. If Delta went under, Hartsfield would be in big trouble. The tonnage of cargo handled is meanwhile expected to increase still more sharply. Beginning in 1925 as an aerodrome with a dirt racetrack as runway, it has grown organically to its present form – the now almost iconic four-runway, midfield-terminal layout, masterplanned as early as 1966. It has one main landside terminal and six subsidiary concourses with 168 gates, all amounting to just a fraction less covered area than Denver. Perhaps as a consequence of its compact plan and its closeness to town, it is not utterly dependent on cars but also has a busy rail transit station. The rail system will be extended to a new south terminal, which alone will cost $1.8 billion.

Hartsfield's 1966 ground plan, with its ultra-logical configuration of main terminal followed by an echelon of successive subsidiary concourses linked by a transit system, all set within the runway system, has proved enormously influential. Denver copied it. The huge expansion now planned for hideously congested Washington Dulles airport – with Saarinen's original terminal already preserved and deftly extended in the same idiom by SOM – follows the same plan of a main terminal followed by a succession of smaller concourses like

This page Chicago O'Hare's United Airlines terminal, 1983–7, by Murphy/Jahn Architects. Like London's Heathrow, O'Hare is struggling to expand on a limited site.

waves breaking on a beach. KPF is designing the new midfield concourse. London Heathrow's new Terminal 5 by Richard Rogers, which is intended to make it possible to handle another 30 million passengers each year, is also essentially the Hartsfield terminal-and-waves-of-concourses plan. So is Rogers's new terminal at Barajas airport, Madrid (with Estudio Lamela), which is another huge project, begun in 1997, that will double Madrid's capacity to 70 million a year. This being Europe, both Barajas and Terminal 5 will have a full provision of rail and metro links. In London this is in pursuit of the aim of the operator, BAA plc, to have half or more of its non-connecting passengers using public transport. Heathrow invested a total of £6 billion ($9.8 billion) in rebuilding itself in the years either side of the turn of the century, involving the large-scale remodelling and extension of its existing terminals by Rogers, Nicholas Grimshaw and others, as well as the all-new and enormous Terminal 5. The sum of £6 billion could have built an entirely new international airport, but instead, these major works could be seen as effectively the last gasp of a landlocked London airport that has reached capacity with its two main runways and has none of Denver's huge landholding to fall back on. But Heathrow, like Amsterdam's Schipol, which was undergoing similar expansion at this time to a masterplan by architects Benthem Crouwel, has shown an extraordinary ability to absorb extra traffic. Although London is now thinking about extra runways not so much at Heathrow as anywhere in the southeast of England – and despite the fact that government economists were factoring the eventual closure of Heathrow into their long-term planning even before Terminal 5 started to be built – Heathrow cannot yet be regarded as a completed project.

Nor, even though a new Parisian airport is being discussed, can Paris Charles de Gaulle yet be regarded as built out. The airport is increasingly referred to as Roissy after the area north of Paris where it was built from 1967 to 1974, with near-continuous later phases. Roissy is thus contemporary with Atlanta, but it has little in common with its giant American cousin, being built to a completely different configuration. It shows more of the influence of other American airports being built around that time, notably the circular terminal configuration of Kansas City International by Kivett and Myers (1968–72) and the hemispherical layout of terminals, divided by service roads, of Dallas-Fort Worth by TAMS and HOK (1965–73). Roissy is much more tightly planned than either of these, and it is a bit of a futile argument to say which came first, but it is possible to see Kansas in the circular Roissy 1 terminal, and Dallas in the sequence of half-oval buildings of Roissy 2, which has the same arrangement of a central spine service road.

This page The new Barajas airport by Richard Rogers and Partners with Estudio Lamela, 1997–2006. The high-tech shed goes organic.

Above Design for the first phase (1989–2008) of Terminal 5, London Heathrow, by Richard Rogers and Partners. The scheme was value-engineered into a much simpler form that the original competition-winning scheme of 1989 (above). It will handle 30 million passengers a year.

Right and below Original competition-winning scheme of 1989 for Terminal 5, London.

All pictures Dallas-Fort Worth, by
TAMS and HOK, 1965–73.
Hemispherical terminals are divided by
a central transport spine. An influence
on later phases of Paris Roissy?

The opening of Roissy in 1974 (see pages 156–9) ended the story of Le
Bourget – already eclipsed by Orly – as Paris's historic point of departure and
arrival. Le Bourget continues as a venue for air shows and private aviation, and
as a museum of flight, which has preserved the 1930s buildings. However, the
first instalment of Roissy proved to be a complete break with tradition. Where Le
Bourget and Orly were both linear terminals, Paul Andreu at the Aeroports de
Paris (ADP) architecture department revisited the 1930s idea of the circular
terminal as exemplified by the original London Gatwick. What he made was a
condensed version of the land-hungry doughnut layout of Kansas, but with
important modifications. The great discus of Roissy 1, raised high on branching
concrete columns, is, depending on the metaphor adopted, a citadel or a
spaceship. It contains parking space but, unlike the huge doughnut terminals of
Kansas, it does not give over the space in the middle to surface car lots. Instead,
the surprisingly small central space – really just a conical lightwell – becomes a
dramatic place of transition, a zone of light and dancing fountains, which
passengers can see but not touch as they travel across it on their Travelator in
their Plexiglass tube. As they do, they notice other passengers criss-crossing the
space in their respective tubes, going somewhere else, like astronauts to the
launch pad. It was and is a masterly *coup de théâtre*, particularly given that the
next stage of the journey has passengers plunging underground, beneath the
apron, to one of the seven roughly triangular satellite concourses, which are
placed symmetrically around the main building. The whole layout was derived
from a free-flowing circulation pattern that also allows planes to exit the runway
on landing at high speed before spiralling in to the relevant satellite. This feature
– along with the fact that the whole airport was designed from the first to
accommodate the then-new Boeing 747 – makes it particularly efficient in terms
of throughput.

What, then, made Andreu and ADP abandon the circular model – originally
intended to be duplicated several times as the airport expanded – in favour of
the sliced-watermelon layout of Roissy 2? Certainly, the doughnut plan of the
first terminal, for all its moon-age drama, had drawbacks. As with all terminals of
this type – Berlin's hexagonal Tegel is another example – it is easy for
passengers to get disorientated and to lose track of where they are on the
circumference. When it is not immediately clear – especially when they are late
for a plane – which direction passengers take, there is something awry. ADP's
clear signage helps, but a terminal should ideally be self-explanatory. Moreover,
the system of central terminal and more distant satellite concourses means that
the distance between the arrival point and plane can be quite great, and the
moving-walkways system only partly compensates for this.

For all these reasons, plus a desire to have a more efficient service-road
system bisecting what would originally have been a series of circular terminals,
the decision was made to shift Roissy to the Dallas-Fort Worth model, although,
of course, greatly compacted, this being Europe. Andreu being Andreu, the model
was transformed into something quite other, much more urban, akin to a
sequence of grand classical crescents, each one numbered – Terminal 2a, 2b
and so on. The end result is almost like a linear terminal, only with undulating
edges, so allowing more planes to plug in. Then came the grand gesture of the

Above Paris Roissy (Charles de Gaulle, or CDG) adopted the spine-and-hemisphere layout after its first, circular phase.

Opposite Most recently Roissy has sprouted broad tapering 'peninsulas' to provide extra gates and more passenger facilities. The airport world was traumatised on 23 May 2004, when a 30-metre section of pier at Roissy's newest terminal, 2e, suddenly collapsed, killing four people. The terminal was closed as an urgent inquiry was launched into what could have caused such an unprecedented structural failure.

high-speed train station, slicing across the spine of the terminal and expressed as a tectonic movement, the steel and glass station structure, engineered by the great Peter Rice, piling up on either side of the central spine road. Paris is fortunate in that both of its airports, Orly and Roissy, are on the rapid rail link (as is Disneyland, Paris). As with all the latest generation of European and Far Eastern airports, the idea is that the airport becomes a portal not just to a city or a region, but also internationally. Passengers can arrive by plane at Roissy and take a fast train to all the key European centres. At such hubs they have the choice of connecting to their onward journey, either by air or by rail. Big cities are sufficiently close in most of Europe – as they are on the eastern seaboard of the United States – to make this choice a realistic one.

The second terminal at Roissy continued to develop as Andreu laid out the segments one by one on either side of the spine road. By the time he got to the fifth segment, numbered 2f (2e came later), it was time for another reassessment. Section 2f was the first one beyond the new station, and Andreu here devised a plan that was more compact, efficient and user friendly. The segment sprouted two, fat, boat-shaped piers, which he calls 'peninsulas'; these give passengers much more space and many more facilities, such as shops and restaurants, while they are in the last stage before disembarking. Like great glass conservatories, these public spaces have a sense of space and light that was previously absent in many such airports, particularly on the upper level. No doubt the increasing importance of retail in airports contributed to the planning, since the comparison with the tight little satellites at Roissy 1 is telling. What had previously been relatively basic holding-pens for passengers in the last stage of processing before boarding has become an altogether more generous and relaxed – and, of course, income-generating – affair. This makes sense for customers as well as the operator. One of the great disappointments of modern air travel is the one-way system of people processing that leaves passengers at the end of the line, near the departure gate but stuck in an austere lounge with time to kill and nothing to do unless they fight their way back through the system – something that increased security makes increasingly difficult to do. With the opening of the mirror-image section of Terminal 2e, this latest two-segment phase of Roissy offers the same passenger space as the previous four segments. Being partially separated from them by the railway station complex with its associated buildings, it can be regarded as a new terminal in itself.

Several commentators have remarked on the geometric and symmetrical nature of Andreu's approach, which may be seen at airports designed by ADP around the world. Although this approach is by no means confined to him and may be said to be generated at least partly by the fluid dynamics of aircraft and people movements, it is nonetheless clear that this is urban planning of a historical kind, not just the classically inspired Beaux Arts tradition but also analogous to the designers of utopias – ideal cities – from the 16th century on. It is certainly true that airport planning represents one of the few areas today in which architects and landscape designers can start with a blank page and sketch out a combined townscape and landscape on a grand scale. With a large number of jobs provided, with maintenance and repair depots akin to factories, with a large number of service industries, with many hotel rooms, places to eat and

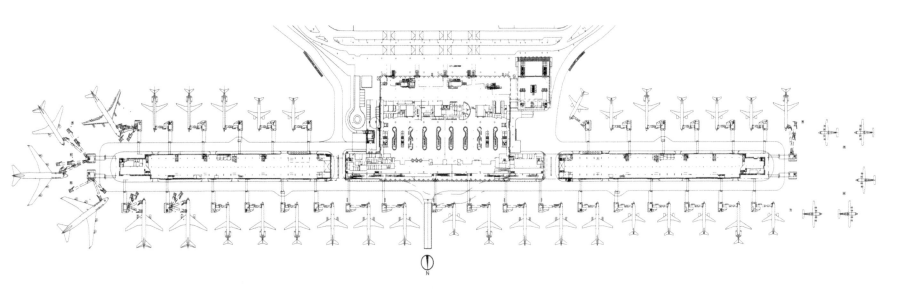

shop, places of worship and advanced transport systems designed to
accommodate very large numbers of people, the design of an airport is
masterplanning writ large. All it really lacks are schools and time-consuming
entertainment, like cinemas, which are the province of the planes rather than the
terminals. Nor can such enterprises be allowed to fail. The economic importance
of these places to the wider economy of region and nation is just too great. To
design such a place is consequently a sobering responsibility.

To have a blank page to start from in Europe is a comparatively rare luxury,
although it happens periodically. The new Athens-Spata airport, Eleftherios
Venizelos, opened in 2001 in readiness for the 2004 Olympic Games. It cost €2.5
billion ($2.4 billion), was the biggest infrastructure project Greece had ever
undertaken and is as dull as the far larger Paris-Roissy or Denver are interesting.
There is the twin-runway configuration, there is the central service road, there is
the linear terminal set to one side of it, and (at the time of opening) a single
satellite concourse at a distance, set at right angles to it. A commercial
development is planned to fill in most of the rest of the land between the two
widely spaced runways. Unusually for a brand-new airport, it was opened with a
surprising number of remote plane stands – nearly two-thirds of the total. This
may partly have been in response to the low-charge ethos of the budget holiday
airlines, but it was the first Greek airport ever to have airbridges at all.

It works well enough. It was opened with a six-lane highway connection and
was due to get its rail link in time for the Olympics, but even as a diagram it lacks
the beauty of the better airport layouts, while the architecture of the terminal
buildings is particularly lacklustre. Inside the main terminal concourse, with air-
handling ducts and lighting rigs hanging from the ceiling, it is like a throwback to
the less-inspired airports of the 1970s and 1980s. This probably reflects the fact
that the whole airport was designed and built very quickly (a 51-month
construction period) by an international conglomerate turnkey contractor in a
public-private partnership of the type concerned with time and cost rather than
aesthetics. Athens wants to be like Barcelona and become a key hub for the
northern Mediterranean. It has a way to go. Athens was, in architectural terms, an
opportunity missed just as surely as Oslo's Gardermoen, a national gateway
airport for Norway opened in 1998, was an opportunity grasped.

The two airports are of similar size. Gardermoen, too, represented the largest
infrastructure project ever for its host nation. Designed by the Aviaplan
consortium with architect Niels Torp (b.1940) as a key consultant, it is better in
terms of layout, aesthetics and environmental awareness. Historically,
Gardermoen also slots into airport history in being, like Berlin's Tempelhof and a
number of other early airports, built on what was originally a military parade
ground – or more accurately, a military exercise zone that had evolved to include
an airbase. Designed to double in size with relative ease – tunnels were put in
place under the runways so that future construction traffic could operate with
minimum disruption – it was also the first of a new breed of airport terminal to be
cooled in summer and warmed in winter by means of thermal storage using
ground water, so cutting out the usual colossal energy consumption of such
places. Although its design plan is conventionally familiar – the central terminal
with wave-form roof, flanked by longitudinal piers, giving a total length of 820m

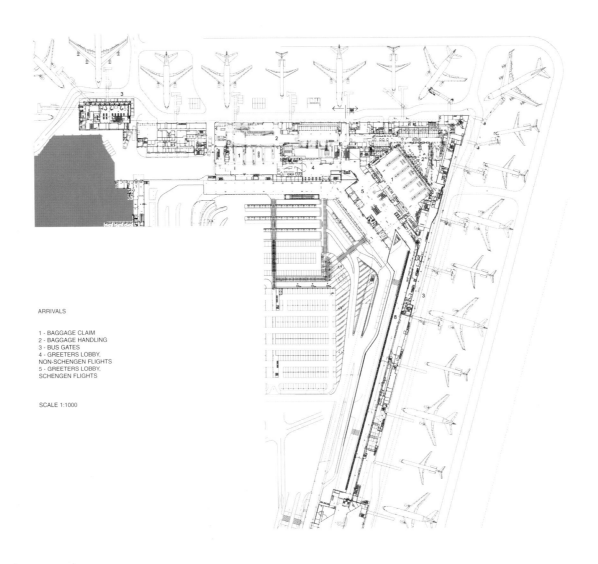

ARRIVALS

1 - BAGGAGE CLAIM
2 - BAGGAGE HANDLING
3 - BUS GATES
4 - GREETERS LOBBY,
NON-SCHENGEN FLIGHTS
5 - GREETERS LOBBY,
SCHENGEN FLIGHTS

SCALE 1:1000

(2,690ft), it is done in a spirit of innovation. This is particularly apparent in its use of paired, long-span, laminated timber beams, engineered by Arup, which recall to some extent the timber trusses of early aircraft hangars. Other natural materials appropriate to the region give it a warm, almost domestic feel.

Torp did not try to reinvent the airport terminal – there is a lot of Meinhard von Gerkan's Stuttgart, not to mention ADP and Renzo Piano's Kansai (of which more later) and Foster's Stansted in the genes of the building, while the overall layout closely resembles Munich. Once again, the aim is diagrammatic clarity. Perhaps as a nod to the heroic era of pre-war airport design, the control tower – very tall and slender, and inclined to sway (a little alarmingly at times for those in there for the first time) – is brought into the terminal composition. It is placed just behind the main building, although just off-axis in the modern manner. Needless to say, a rail terminal, for inter-city travel as well as fast trips into Oslo, also tucks in behind, while the road loop drops passengers off at virtually the same point. There is nothing ill thoughtout or unconsidered about Gardermoen. It demonstrates that an airport can be civilized and civic minded. This is the Scandinavian way, which is to be seen in other such congenial places as Copenhagen and Helsinki-Vantaa. Copenhagen now has its new Terminal 3 and station by the indefatigable Lauritzen practice, the two connected by a triangular concourse with delta-wing (or paper dart) roof. Helsinki-Vantaa, with its latest terminal by Pekka Salminen architects, has a highly unusual triangulated plan generated by the intersection of two runways. The best place to be there is in the restaurant at the very apex of the building, which affords views of both runways.

All pictures Helsinki-Vantaa middle
terminal, 1994–9. It has an unusual
triangulated plan on the corner of the
two runways. The plan (opposite)
shows the arrivals area.

Helsinki-Vantaa is significant as an airport that openly embraces the fact that it is a city in itself. The airport proper is not in the world's mega-league, and the Helsinki metropolitan area, consisting of four adjacent cities, has a population of fewer than a million inhabitants in total. But despite – or because of – this relatively small-scale hinterland, the city of Vantaa sees itself as the airport, while the airport is seen as a generator of urban fabric. The city fathers declare: 'The Airport City may be understood, depending on the context, as the entire City of Vantaa, or as the business areas in the vicinity of the international Helsinki-Vantaa airport. The airport influences the development of the City of Vantaa in many ways. The road links to the airport form an important basis for the planning of the street network, while housing can only be built outside the aircraft noise zones. The airport is also Vantaa's largest area of workplaces and attracts many different businesses.'

That this should be the case demonstrates admirably joined-up thinking. Airports are too often regarded as forces of nature or as natural disasters, depending on one's viewpoint. They are like cuckoos in the metropolitan nest, dumped there by unthinking parents, soon to outgrow and destroy their surroundings. But those who take the view that an airport should be planned into metropolitan design thinking from the outset allow a different outcome. This attitude is to be found in Vienna, where the authorities drew up a masterplan in 1998 to take their airport to 2015 with separate architectural competitions for a new airport terminal, for the control tower, for an office park and for the buildings of a new dedicated airport express link to the centre – only the fourth such wholly dedicated airport rail link in the world after the examples at London's Heathrow and Gatwick, and Hong Kong's Airport Express Line. Other airports with rail connections generally use trains that are also going elsewhere. The key investment is €414 ($525) million, which will be spent by 2008 on the new sickle-shaped, northeast terminal. The competition winners there are architects Baumschlager Eberle with Itten and Brechbühl. Zechner and Zechner are designing the 109m (358ft) control tower, a massive lighthouse-like structure, very different from the slender wands more common today, which fulfilled the stated desire of the airport company 'to build a unique architectural structure, and thereby create a new landmark for the region surrounding the airport'. The whole masterplan is thus seen in regional terms, taking in urban areas well outside the airport's boundary.

A similar urbanistic spirit, though expressed in far more commercial terms, is to be found at Amsterdam's Schipol, which its operators now describe thus: 'Schipol Group views an airport as an AirportCity: a dynamic hub integrating people and companies, logistics and shops, information and entertainment.'

Note that there is no mention of flying people anywhere. In fact, the group is at pains to point out that when it says 'hub', it does not mean that in the airline sense: even though Schipol is, of course, also a hub in the airline sense. This slice of corporate-speak results from the oft-noted fact that by the 1990s airports, particularly in Europe, were earning more money out of retailing than they were out of charging airlines fees to land and take off there. The game instead became a game of adding value. Schipol, in successive waves of enlargement, had long since lost its simple, almost ideogram-like ground plan so

reminiscent of a plane or a standing human figure. It had developed a hugely distended upper body and head in its battle to remain not just a world-class international airport but also a single-terminal airport, despite its size. Architects Benthem Crouwel with Netherlands Airport Consultants (NACO) direct the urban design of the airport, which tripled in capacity in the 15 years from 1986 to 2001 as part of an expansion programme running through to 2005. Key to this was the creation in 1995 of 'Schipol Plaza', essentially a landside shopping mall, predicated on the notion that people might well wish to go there to meet, shop and eat without having to give themselves the excuse of catching a flight.

Consequently, the airport, with its excellent transport links of all kinds, became the equivalent of an out-of-town mall. Like such a development, it also became an area to landscape, and landscape architects West 8 accordingly instigated a programme of rapidly planting the entire area with silver birch trees – the tree that, across northern Europe, is most likely to sprout from odd corners of neglected land and so can flourish well in adverse conditions.

The Dutch would feel at home with an unusual project conceived for the enlargement of Dubai International in the Gulf. In addition to the Future Plan to expand it for A380 superliners by 2006 – a programme led by ADP and Dar Al Handasah – the scheme includes a 'flower centre'. This will not be the usual kiosk, but a mechanized flower-growing factory within the airport, designed by Shairs and Partners as a public spectacle while using the spare land productively.

Such design and landscape programmes help people to feel good about their airports, even if the cynic might dismiss them as mere window-dressing. In the case of Madrid's new Rogers-designed Barajas terminal – which is also, as such places must now be, a mighty transport interchange – sitting the buildings in the landscape, tucking them back into rising ground, keeping the forms low and undulating and designing them to have assisted natural ventilation is now all part of the package, thought through from the first rather than bolted on afterwards. Airports today, in most parts of the developed world, cannot afford to ignore the issue of sustainability.

Below and opposite above Dubai expansion project by ADP/dar Al Handasah. A linear terminal with a sense of scale, scheduled for 2006.

Opposite below Dubai's 'flower center' a mechanized facility for mass-production of blooms.

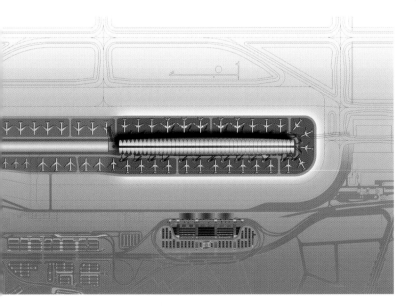

Opposite Pulling an ad-hoc airport
campus together: Grimshaw's low-
energy Airside Center at Zurich, 2003.

This is why the latest expansion of Zurich airport, designed by architects
Grimshaw and engineers Arup, is an exemplar. Claimed to be the first sustainably
engineered airport in Europe, this Swiss project, due to be completed in 2004,
keeps the airport to its 1995 levels of energy use. That might not sound
particularly radical, but it achieves this despite the addition of two very large new
buildings, the Airside Center, 250m (820ft) long and up to 40m (130ft) wide –
much the same scale as the Great Hall of Denver – and a new midfield terminal.
The Airside Centre or Flughafenkopf (airport head) links the two existing
terminals, including the excellent one dating from 1953, with the third as part of
a thorough-going reordering of the airport, which also includes a new bus station,
upgraded rail interchange and shopping centre. In the European way, the old
airport is becoming part of the urban fabric, and the airport, which has much
longer opening hours than most shops in Switzerland, is a resort for shoppers not
flying at all. The national-gateway aspect of such buildings can be overlaid with
another function, one remarkably like a civic square.

An ecologically minded civic programme is equally high on the agenda for the
last big new airport to be planned in Europe for a while, Berlin-Brandenburg. With
the old West German airports of Tempelhof and Tegel and the former East
German airport of Schönefeld, all relatively small, well-planned and, in the case
of the first two, very close to the centre, a new mega-airport for the capital of
reunited Germany will have to work very hard to create the necessary sense of
loyalty. Moreover, Germany has a long tradition of protest on environmental
grounds. The huge expansion of Munich airport – which only opened on its new
site in 1992 and was very quickly overwhelmed – had to tread carefully because
of this. The new Terminal 2 by Koch and Partner, planned on the familiar linear

Right Munich airport, Germany, has expanded hugely since it opened in 1992. The Airport Center, 1989–99, by Murphy/Jahn is the commercial heart of the airport which lies between the two terminals.

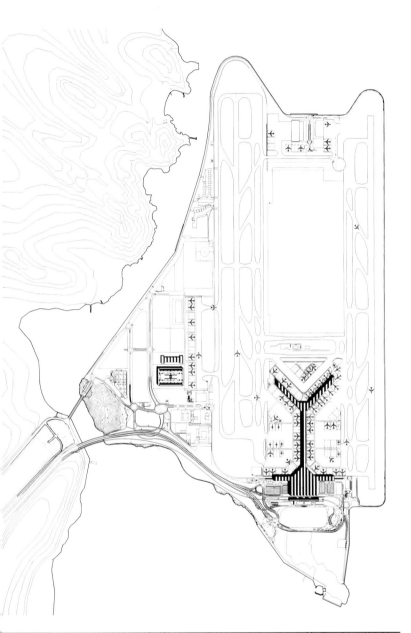

model, was designed and built comparatively rapidly and opened in 2003 with various concessions to the environmental lobby in its design, such as a large power-generating array of photovoltaic cells – enough to power 200 homes, it was said, but not a lot in the context of the power consumption of an airport. Early competition-winning designs by von Gerkan, Marg und Partner for Berlin-Brandenburg International (BBI), which is to be built on the much-expanded Schönefeld site southeast of the city, show once again the familiar template – now an international standard – of terminal with lateral piers linked to a parallel satellite concourse, the whole complex forming the head of a transport system incorporating a central spine of railway and road loop, which, in turn, is flanked by an airport city of large regimented buildings. The big novelty in this design is to make the link between the main terminal and satellite in the form of a dramatic high-level pedestrian bridge, with planes passing beneath, rather than the usual subterranean access.

Although much public consultation was needed – in addition to environmental issues, BBI means relocating one complete village and part of another – the process was not nearly so protracted as it was with Heathrow's Terminal 5, where the design of the terminal was almost incidental compared with the huge bureaucratic public-inquiry exercise that had to be gone through, which lasted for years before the inevitable approval to the project was given. Architect Norman Foster, observing from the sidelines and remembering similarly agonizing delays getting London Stansted built, famously remarked that Britain could have built Terminal 5 for the cost of the public inquiry into it. It was an exaggeration, of course, but there was much truth in the claim.

Even this, however, was preferable to the shambles surrounding the expansion of Russia's largest, and Moscow's main, airport, Sheremetyevo. Notorious for its slow service and grim staff (and that is the opinion of Russians, not foreigners) the twin-terminal, state-run airport, which had not been updated since the Moscow Olympic Games of 1980, found itself becoming increasingly antiquated and overcrowded by the turn of the century. As a result, it started losing airlines and passengers to the privately managed Domodedovo airport on the other side of the city. A rescue plan was drawn up, spearheaded by Aeroflot, which needed international-standard facilities to gain entry to the prestigious Delta-led SkyTeam airline alliance. World-class airport project management expertise was signed up. The project involves a $300m new Terminal 3, designed by Aeroports de Paris in a T-shaped configuration not unlike the projected Barcelona 2. In addition, the present international Terminal 2 would be remodelled and expanded by 30 per cent. All this would turn Sheremetyevo into the largest airport hub between Europe and Asia. Planned to be complete by March 2003, by that date absolutely nothing had happened and two of the airport directors had been fired amid allegations of corruption. The *Moscow Times*, which has followed the affair with mordant humour, noted that the only new facility on which work had started was a small VIP terminal for President Putin and visiting dignitaries, costing £2 ($3) million. In the meantime, Sheremetyevo was haemorrhaging business, losing clients such as British Airways to Domodedovo, which had doubled the size of its 1964 terminal by 2003 and saw its throughput leap by 73 per cent as a consequence of this.

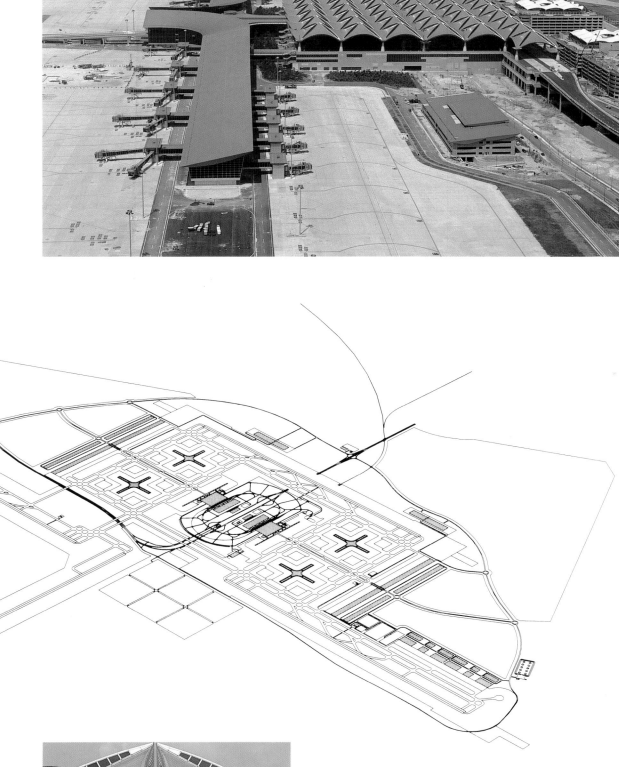

This page Opened at a fraction of its planned eventual size, Malaysia's Kuala Lumpur is built in rainforest and takes its inspiration from trees. The axonometric shows its ambitious plan, with two back-to-back terminals and four cruciform satellites: by Kisho Kurokawa, 1998 (phase one).

Opposite Designed for huge expansion, the site plan of Hong Kong's Chek Lap Kok, by Foster and Partners, 1998, shows how the design resembles a giant plane. Built on reclaimed land, this established the future of the Asian airport. The interior arrivals hall shows its lofty vaulted internal spaces (below).

Overleaf The heart of Kuala Lumpur's first built satellite contains a garden.

All pictures Incheon International
airport, Seoul, Korea, opened in 2001.
The passenger terminal is by Fentress
Bradburn. The transport interchange is
by Terry Farrell.

All pictures The sweeping form of
Kansai airport, Japan, 1994 (Renzo
Piano and ADP) became a symbol of
the new, architecturally ambitious
international terminal.

No such scandals attended the gestation of Berlin-Brandenburg, apart from a surprisingly late decision to bring the project back into the state sector after a preliminary flirtation with private operation. If it is built according to von Gerkan's designs, Berlin will be in the unusual position of having both its airport and its linked city-centre railway station, the Lehrter Bahnhof, designed by the same architect. The schedule was that the new BBI would receive permission by 2004, that Tempelhof would close that year, that BBI would be open for business by 2010, and that Tegel would close six months after that. Thus a long chapter in aviation, going back to Tempelhof's link with the Wright Brothers, came to an end.

The most explosive growth in new airports as the 20th century became the 21st century was in neither America nor Europe, but in the Far East. Here the four key airports are Japan's Kansai (opened 1994), by ADP/Renzo Piano Building Workshop; China's Chek Lap Kok in Hong Kong (1998) by Foster and Partners; Malaysia's Kuala Lumpur International (1998) by Kisho Kurokawa; and Korea's Incheon for the capital, Seoul (2001) by Fentress Bradburn with Terry Farrell for the transport interchange. Hong Kong, Seoul and Kansai were all built on reclaimed land – in the case of Kansai, on a man-made island in the Bay of Osaka. Kurokawa's was set deep in the tropical jungle. Happily for our comparative purposes, each of the four assumed a different shape, so proving that there is still plenty of room for experimentation at the largest scale in this century-old building type.

Kansai is the most extreme example so far built of the linear terminal, the apotheosis of the Paris Orly plan of 1962, a result of master-planner Paul Andreu's decision to have one combined building rather than separate domestic and international terminals, as is often the case. Piano agreed with the concept and, on winning the architectural competition, turned it into what is by common consent one of the great public spaces of the world. Hong Kong, which has equally stupendous spaces but arranged very differently, adopted an aeroplane-shaped ground plan not dissimilar to the Schipol of the mid-1960s. Kuala Lumpur is a central rectangular terminal like a hugely enlarged Stansted, with a remote cruciform satellite and expansion space to add three more. And Incheon is a hemispherical plan with two projecting wings, in concept not so dissimilar from the most recent phases of Andreu's Paris Roissy.

How does one relate all these places to each other? Scale is one common factor, self-containment another. All are virtual city-states, all send tendrils of development corridors shooting off towards their respective cities, all are hubs, all are designed with rail links, all are planned to expand greatly. Even Kansai, on its rectangular island, can be extended, for the island can be enlarged and a second terminal built. Hong Kong and Incheon have both already reclaimed enough land to allow for future expansion. At Kuala Lumpur the airport is part of a masterplan involving a business district of high-tech industries and a new government administrative centre nearby. Moreover, all four embrace the aesthetic of the superscale public gathering-place with lightweight, relatively unencumbered roofs, which are so different from the low, suspended ceilings and maze of ductwork familiar to us from the era of frantic airport expansion from the 1960s to the 1980s.

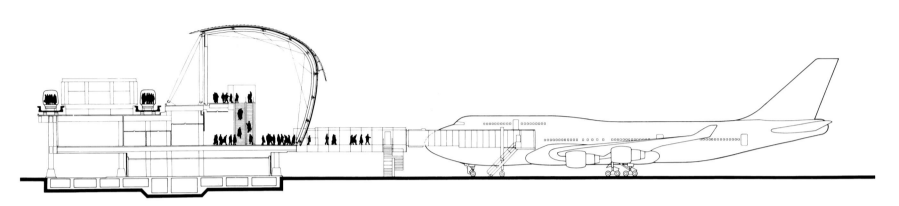

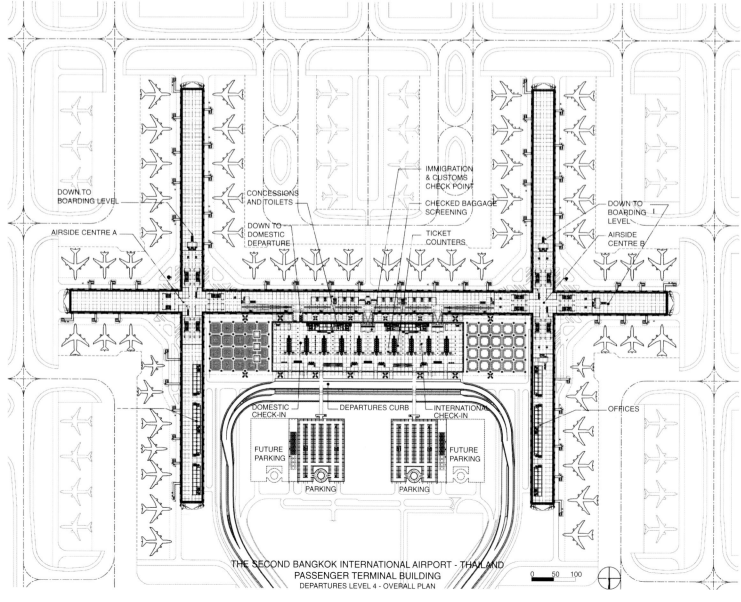

DOWN TO
BOARDING LEVEL

CONCESSIONS
AND TOILETS

IMMIGRATION
& CUSTOMS
CHECK POINT

CHECKED BAGGAGE
SCREENING

DOWN TO
BOARDING
LEVEL

AIRSIDE CENTRE A

DOWN TO
DOMESTIC
DEPARTURE

TICKET
COUNTERS

AIRSIDE
CENTRE B

DOMESTIC
CHECK-IN

DEPARTURES CURB

INTERNATIONAL
CHECK-IN

OFFICES

FUTURE
PARKING

FUTURE
PARKING

PARKING

PARKING

THE SECOND BANGKOK INTERNATIONAL AIRPORT - THAILAND
PASSENGER TERMINAL BUILDING
DEPARTURES LEVEL 4 - OVERALL PLAN

0   50   100

Below Model of Bangkok's new
Savarnabhumi airport by Murphy/Jahn,
TAMS and ACT, scheduled for 2005.

Opposite The colossal temple-like
roof (above) and tubular concourses
of Bangkok's departures and
passenger terminal building. The
double-T plan (below) has an annual
capacity of 100 million. Will the
people come?

The irony is that these huge airports with their vast expansion potential were opened at a sustained moment of pause in the airline business. They arrived in time for an economic recession in the Far East, followed by the industry-crippling fear of terrorist attack after the 2001 assault on New York's World Trade Center and the subsequent outbreak of the much-feared SARS virus, which particularly affected the Asia-Pacific region. So for a while, the growth projections in air travel for the region and the grand airport plans drawn up to accommodate them seemed highly over-optimistic. To this could be added the fear of over-capacity at rival airports. As a Southeast Asian hub, for instance, ambitious Kuala Lumpur found itself in competition with the new Bangkok international airport, Suvarnabhumi. With its double-T terminal layout by Murphy/Jahn, TAMS and ACT, its spectacular, raised, temple-like main terminal roof and giant, tubular, lightweight concourses, it was due for completion in September 2005. Brasher than Kurokawa's admittedly dramatic but more sophisticated design, Suvanrabhumi is due to open with a capacity of 45 million passengers, with expansion room for 100 million. Quite some rival, but it is not the only one. Singapore's Changi is even nearer to Kuala Lumpur and is in the process of doubling in size, with a new Terminal 3 by SOM, built at a cost of $1.5 billion, due to open in 2006 under one of the world's great roofs. This is a 220m (720ft) long by 4m (13ft) deep, steel truss-supported roof with 1,100 skylights and 215,000 cable-supported, perforated aluminium louvres, all in the cause of reflecting and diffusing the tropical sunlight of the region. It is a very different response to Kurokawa's sequence of grand structural 'trees' supporting domes with interstitial skylights and to the Murphy/Jahn complex truss system at Bangkok, but the upshot is the same in travel terms: Singapore is another big, world-class hub airport – it has an eventual capacity of 64 million passengers – relatively close to two others of similar capacity in Southeast Asia. How these fervent expressions of competitive national pride settle down with each other is anyone's guess, but it looks like a buyer's market for airlines.

Australia's international airports have been growing, most notably at Sydney, with terminals by Woodhead International and Bligh Voller Nield and control tower – one of the more outré examples going – by Ancher/Mortlock/Wooley. But the big player in the Pacific Rim continues to be China. The rapid rate of airport building and rebuilding there at first looks puzzling, since there is no competing national pride involved. But only part of this expansion is due to the opening up to international trade and tourism. At many Chinese airports the international section is small. What it is to do with is the modernization of China itself and, in particular, the freeing-up of restrictions on internal travel. The Civil Aviation Administration of China (CAAC) conceived the idea of a series of relatively small new domestic terminals across the country and a few big international centres – Shanghai, Beijing, Guangzhou – plus the new ex-colonial airports of the trading outposts of Hong Kong and Macau.

Shanghai-Pudong, by the ubiquitous Paul Andreu of ADP, adopts the familiar Kansai linear-terminal plan – with the addition of glazed bowspring-truss aerofoil roofs somewhat reminiscent, in their more delicate way, of Saarinen's TWA terminal at New York JFK. The first phase opened in 1999, but the key thing

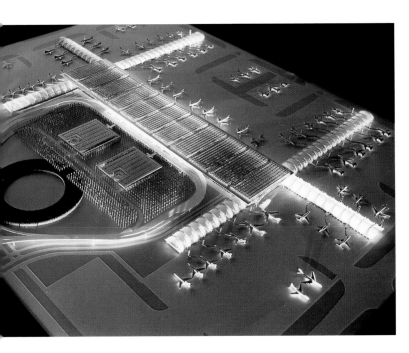

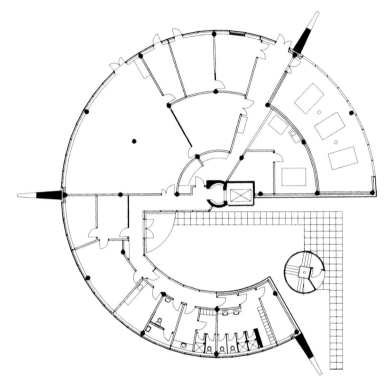

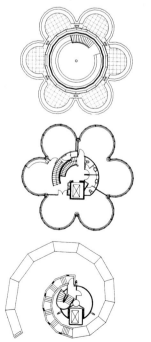

Above Acting as campanile to the 1961 'Theme building', the control tower by Kate Diamond of Siegel Diamond, 1995, at Los Angeles International airport.

Opposite Control tower fantasia the Sydney control tower by Ancher/Mortlock/Woolley, 1995.

about the design is the way it is designed to expand fourfold, finishing as the equivalent of two sets of Kansais, back-to-back, each 1,370m (4,500ft) long. Kansai is admittedly longer at 1,700m (5,577ft, more than a mile) long. The Shanghai-Pudong project is a grand axial plan on a staggering scale, but remember, even when it is fully built out, it will still process only 70 million passengers a year, by which time hemmed-in Atlanta Hartsfield will allegedly be up to 121 million. It is, however, typical of the forward planning of airports in China, where anything but a short-term view is taken. Instead, the planning is done for 30–50 years hence, and international architectural competitions for the terminals is normal. Mayors and vice-mayors of provinces regard these as projects that bring prestige as well as trade to their regions. At the same time a whole generation of Chinese architects and planners is being trained in the specialist arts of airport-making. At Xian Xianyang, for instance, the city that is a big tourist centre because of the archaeological wonder of the 'terracotta army', a 50-year masterplan has been drawn up, with Llewelyn-Davies as consultants, involving not just the airport, but a complete business district.

At the time of writing, the biggest Chinese competition of all was for a large new terminal at Beijing Capital International airport, valued at $2 billion to be built in time for the Olympic Games there in 2008 and subsequently planned to get much larger. In typical Chinese fashion, it is intended to be enlarged to a

Below The Berlin-Brandenburg
International by von Gerkan, Marg and
Partner, 1998–2010, features a 25m
(82ft) high passenger bridge linking
the main and satellite terminals.

Opposite The new terminal 3 at
Beijing Capital International, 2003–8,
by Foster and Partners with NACO
and Arup, supplies the single-building
solution to the 21st-century airport.

120-gate capacity, with railway interchange, by 2020. In the past the hardest-fought architectural competitions were always for cultural buildings. Today, airports have an equal pull. Some 17 international practices were long-listed for the Beijing competition, subsequently refined down to three: ADP from France, Foster and Partners from Britain and Yang Molmen from the US, with German engineers Meinhardt. Foster won it in 2003.

It remains to be seen just how mega the world's mega-airports can become. Building from scratch is one thing but, as Heathrow demonstrates, it is harder work dealing with existing cramped airports. Similar American examples include Washington National by Cesar Pelli with Leo A. Daly, Chicago O'Hare by Murphy/Jahn, Gensler and others, Seattle-Tacoma by Fentress Bradburn and NBBJ, McCarran airport Las Vegas by Tate Snyder and Kimsey – the list seems practically endless. Most of the world's older airports are still catching up with the late 20th century rather than anticipating the needs of the 21st century. How much more building can be squeezed on to them before it is time to draw a line under a historic site and move somewhere else? That raises the question of what kind of airport will be needed in 20, 30 or 50 years' time. To that question, as we shall see next, there is an intriguing variety of possible answers.

There are numerous possible futures for the airport as a phenomenon of the built environment. Some are more likely than others, some are more science fiction than others, some depend on unprovable assumptions about changing social and economic trends. Here are six possible scenarios.

Future One – More and Bigger

The trend established in the first century of airport development continues, albeit with hiccups, into the second. This future looks at the past, sees how air travel has always grown faster than expectations and observes that airliner design is more stable, conservative and predictable than ever. It notes those regions of the world, such as the Far East, Africa, South America and the former Soviet Bloc, that are not yet mature markets and lag behind the more developed world in terms of the percentage of their populations frequently travelling by air. It statistically removes the blips caused by war, terrorism, disease epidemics and economic recessions and projects the graph forwards to show a steady-to-fast upward growth trend. It is on this future that the world's newer mega-airports, with their vast potential for expansion, are planned and built. We know what such airports will look like because they and their terminals are already designed, in some cases through to 2030. This argument is inductive rather than deductive: it cannot imagine radically different circumstances. One remembers the forecasts of the environmentally disastrous growth of urban horse traffic at the end of the 19th century.

Endnote Six Futures

Future Two – Hiatus

The downturn in air travel following the terrorist destruction of the World Trade Center in New York on 11 September 2001 turns out to be no mere blip on the graph. Followed by a global economic retrenchment and a basket of other disincentives to travel, enough large and small airlines and aircraft-makers merge or go out of business to reduce capacity significantly. Competition is reduced and prices rise, then rise some more when the nations of the world finally get serious about global pollution and start to tax jet fuel, hence travel. The era of cheap air travel is over. The upshot is that passenger numbers do not grow at anything like the rate predicted. Air travel becomes once more the preserve of the better-off. This, coupled with the greater use of fewer, larger planes, reduces the pressure of volume on the world's airports, so leading to a pause in building around the world. Ambitious expansion and new-build plans are curtailed or abandoned. Like railway stations from the 1920s onwards, airport terminals stop growing and enter a steady state. People start to refer nostalgically to a second golden era of the architecture of flight, the turn of the 21st century.

Future Three – Deus ex Machina

A new wonder transport system is devised. This might be an improved form of otherwise relatively conventional supersonic high-flying airliner. It might be an enormous ground-and-sea hugging aircraft of the kind some predict as cargo-carriers to supercede conventional shipping. It might be a sub-orbital shuttle that adopts much the same trajectory as an intercontinental ballistic missile and so fires people halfway around the world in next to no time at all. It might be the long-predicted, always-delayed reintroduction of the large, luxurious but slow-moving, lighter-than-air airship. Or it might be something else entirely. We do not know because something as desirable as an entirely new cheap, reliable and environmentally benign propulsion system has not yet been invented, though we have certain indicators, such as the potential of hydrogen power. In this future, the new 'disruptive technology' is so good that it renders conventional airliners redundant, and with them the airports that were built to serve them. The faster and larger such transports are, the fewer landing places they require, and those are likely to be very different. Weeds sprout through the cracks in the concrete of the great airports of the world, now abandoned. Vast terminals lie empty and derelict, or continue their logical development into giant shopping malls, business parks and industrial estates, this time with no planes attached.

Future Four – the New Woodlanders

Thomas Hardy's 1887 novel *The Woodlanders* is set among the lives of country folk who scarcely ever leave their own village and then only to walk to the next one through the trees. News from far away finds its way through eventually, scarcely disturbing the tenor of rural life. When the protagonists go off to fancy foreign parts (the intrusion of the modern world), it causes nothing but trouble and misunderstanding, and reconciliation is only possible when the old order is reinvoked. The New Woodlanders will not need or want to travel because all their communications are entirely electronic. Business travel has ceased to exist because of vastly improved virtual-reality video-conferencing and the like, while the greatly increased cost, inconvenience and perceived danger of flying has all but killed off the overseas-holiday trade for the masses. An agrarian revolution, spurred on by the anti-globalization movement, means that food is once more grown close to where it is consumed, rather than being expensively transported long distances. We stop flying all round the world because there is no point any more. Airports wither and die as a consequence, with only token international gateways required. The redundant acres are converted to self-sufficient decentralized communities along the utopian lines of Frank Lloyd Wright's Broadacre City. Deadly global conflict or disease pandemics would hasten this.

Future Five – the Detached Terminal

Airport capacity is about runways and the ability of terminal buildings to process people and to provide, in retail and entertainment terms, an 'experience'. There is no absolute reason why the terminal experience and the people processing need always be sited right next to the runways. Airports such as Heathrow, Zurich and Hong Kong have long had subsidiary check-in points in the city centres. Many large cities already have transport links between their two or three biggest airports for transit passengers, so breaking the connection between runway and associated building. The critic Peter Reyner Banham argued in 1962 that the grand airfield terminal could wither away. It did not, but now perhaps it could. Enhanced just-in-time technology, as used to synchronize the manufacture and delivery of goods, so doing away with the need to keep large stocks, is capable of being adapted to this end. It could manage a much enlarged city-centre terminal (or a cluster or necklace of smaller ones), which would then take passengers via rapid automated transport systems directly to their departure gates at the relevant airport – which, for example, could be as much as 240km (150 miles) away. One such terminal or terminal complex could serve all the airports of a city or region, so allowing all available runways to be used to maximum efficiency. Delayed or diverted flights would matter less if passengers were kept in the city centre, not stuck out at the (possibly wrong) airport. There would thus be no need for the large airfield terminals of the kind to which we have become accustomed. The main weakness of this scenario, apart from its dependence on logistical exactitude, is the high cost of city-centre land compared with land costs at remote airports. But by pooling the resources of several airports, this differential could be resolved.

Future Six – Redispersal

The trend in the second half of the 20th century was for the principal airports of any country or geographical region to get steadily larger, concentrating traffic at the expense of the smaller airfields that used to provide a more dispersed service for smaller planes travelling shorter distances. The 'hub' system, whereby certain airports act as trans-shipment points for huge numbers of passengers, exacerbated this trend. But as the 21st century progresses, spurred on by the low-cost airline revolution, large, congested, centralized airports with their potential for knock-on delay are increasingly shunned by carriers and customers alike. Instead, there is a strong revival of smaller regional airports serving as convenient departure and arrival points for more dispersed populations which are accustomed to relatively short-hop flights. Such handier facilities with their smaller scale, often basic terminal buildings are also given a boost by being needed as satellite runways to the world's intercontinental mega-airports. They act like stations on 19th- and early 20th-century railway branch lines, feeding passengers into the main routes as well as providing a local service. This new breed of regional airport is much faster to build, more environmentally friendly and more popular than the centralized model, which was, anyway, an artificial construct based on either subsidized state airlines or monopolistic private carriers. In both cases, true deregulation of the carriers leads to a greater choice of airports. Architects reprise the model of the small, compact and legible terminal building of the early to mid-20th century.

Conclusion – the Urban Imperative

Of course, the real future for airports is as likely to be an amalgam of any or all of the above. No matter what the outcome, the world's architects and planners are increasingly treating the airport not as a separate entity but as just another part of the urban condition. This approach needs to be taken much further. Airports large or small are always about more than the buildings and infrastructure needed for passengers and planes. They are always a focus for other activities. Like the medieval cathedral, the well-designed airport always attracts its circlet of ill-designed shanties and rookeries. The task now is to design effectively for the whole physical, environmental and emotional experience of the airport over a wide area. That imperative has scarcely begun to be addressed seriously.

Bibliography

Apart from all the individual architects' and single-project monographs, international journal articles, yearbooks and website gleanings that inform a book of this kind, the following books, ancient and modern, in their different ways all illuminate the phenomenon of airport design: some directly, some tangentially:

Banham, Reyner: *A Critic Writes (Selected Essays)*, University of California Press, 1996.

Binney, Marcus: *Airport Builders*, Academy Editions, London, 1999.

Blankenship, Edward G: *The Airport: Architecture, Urban Integration, Ecological Problems*, Pall Mall Press, London, 1974.

Blow, Christopher J: *Airport Terminals*, Butterworth-Heinemann, London 1991.

Christians, G: *Anlage und Betrieb von Luftschiffhafen*, Oldenbourg, Munich, 1914.

Collis, Hugh: *Transport, Engineering and Architecture*, Laurence King, London, 2003.

Corbusier, Le: *Essential Le Corbusier: L'Esprit Nouveau Articles*, Architectural Press, Oxford, 1998.

Corn, Joseph J. (ed): *Imagining Tomorrow: History, Technology and the American Future*, MIT Press, Massachusetts, 1986.

Dean, C. (ed): *Housing the Airship,* Architectural Association, London, 1989.

Edwards, Brian: *The Modern Terminal: New Approaches to Airport Architecture*, E. and F.N. Spon, London, 1998.

Forsyth, Alastair: *Buildings for the Age: New Building Types 1900–1939*, Royal Commission on Historical Monuments, London, 1982.

Glidden, Horace Knight and others: *Airports: Design, Construction and Management*, McGraw-Hill, New York, 1946.

Greif, Martin: *The Airport Book: From Landing Field to Modern Terminal*, Smithmark Publishing, New York 1979.

Hanks, Stedman S: *International Airports*, Ronald Press, New York, 1929.

Horonjeff, R: *Planning and Design of Airports*, McGraw-Hill, New York, 1962–92.

Kazda, Antonin and Caves, Robert E: *Airport Design and Operation*, Pergamon Press, New York, 2000.

Lovegrove, Keith: *Airline: Identity, Design and Culture*, Laurence King, London, 2000.

Pearman, Hugh: *Contemporary World Architecture*, Phaidon, London, 1998.

Peter, John: *The Oral History of Modern Architecture*, Abrams, New York, 2000.

Smith, Paul and Toulier, Bernard (eds): *Berlin-Tempelhof/Liverpool-Speke/Paris-Le Bourget: Airport Architecture of the 1930s*, Editions du Patrimoine/Gingko Press, Paris, 2000.

Veale, Sydney Ernest: *Tomorrow's Airliners, Airways and Airports*, Pilot Press, London, 1945.

Wood, John Walter: *Airports: Some Elements of Design and Future Development*, Coward-McCann, New York, 1940.

Zukowsky, John (ed): *Building for Air Travel: Architecture and Design for Commercial Aviation*, Art Institute of Chicago/Prestel, 1996. (Note: the contributions of Wolfgang Voigt are especially fruitful).

Picture credits

All photographs, drawings and renders are the copyright of the architects or the airport authorities unless otherwise specified.

Aviation Picture Library - APL
British Airways Archives supplied by Adrian Meredith – BAArch
Mary Evans Picture Library – MEPL
Royal Institute of British Architects - RIBA

2/3 Tomio Ohashi; 4 Balthazar Korab; 6/7 AKG London; 8 APL; 9 MEPL; 10 BAArch; 11 MEPL; 12T, 13B The Albuquerque Museum; 12B, 13T MEPL; 14, 15 Angelo Hornak; 16, 17 MEPL; 18T, 19L Flight Collection; 18B Palladium Photodesign; 19R MEPL; 20 BAArch; 21 Flight Collection; 22, 23T, 26/27 © Zeppelin Museum Friedrichschafen; 23B MEPL; 24 Kawatetsu; 28,29b Musée de l'Air et de l'Espace; 29T AKG; 30 MEPL; 31, 32 AKG; 33 Smithsonian Institute; 34T Wright State University Special Collections; 34B MEPL; 35 AKG; 36T MEPL; 36B BPK Erich Mendelsohn Archive, Kunstbibliothek; 37T MEPL; 37B APL; 40T RIBA; 40B National Archives of Australia; 41T Imperial War Museum Q113912; 41B RAF Museum Hendon; 42 MEPL; 43 BAArch; 44 MEPL; 45T Flight Collection; 45B AKG; 46/47 RIBA; 48 BAArch; 49 AKG; 50T MEPL; 50B, 51 BAArch; 52T, 53 APL; 52B Lufthansa Archive; 54 RIBA; 55 AKG; 56 Lockheed Martin Maritime Systems; 57 AKG; 58T MEPL; 58B RIBA; 59 Gandon Editions, Dublin; 60 Farnborough Air Sciences Trust (FAST); 62, 63T RIBA; 63B Reece Winstone Archive/NMR; 64T MEPL; 64B, 65T APL; 65B Musée de l'Air et de l'Aerospace; 66T BAArch; 66B Lufthansa Archive; 67 APL; 68T The Alberqueque Museum; 68M&B, 69B, 70B Lufthansa Archive; 69T APL; 70/71 photo Arne V Peterson, Copenhagen Airports A/S; 72 Historical Museum of Southern Florida; 73, 74T APL; 74B Institut Français d'Architecture; 75 MEPL; 76/77 RIBA; 79 ©ARS, NY and DACS, London, 2004; 80 ©FLC/ADAGP, Paris and DACS, London 2004; 82 WBD Publications © Bob Osborn; 83 RIBA; 84/5 MEPL; 86, 87 Private Collection; 88 ©ARS,NY and DACS, London 2004; 91 Guildhall Library, City of London; 92/3 MEPL; 94 RIBA; 96, 97 MEPL; 98/99 Harry Ransom Humanities Research Center, Austin, Texas ©The Estate of Edith Lutyens Bel Geddes; 99B Megafloat Shipbuilding Research Centre of Japan; 100/101 Balthazar Korab; 102 Gandon Editions, Dublin; 103 APL; 104T MEPL; 104B APL; 105 RIBA; 106 APL; 107T Flight International; 108 BAArch; 109 Dennis Gilbert/View; 110, 111 Nigel Young/Foster & Partners; 112, 113 Tim Hursley; 114, 115 ©Peter Durant/Arcblue.com; 116, 117 BK; 118 Angelo Hornak; 119 BK;121 ©Paul Maurer; 122, 123, 124, 125 Paolo Roselli; 126 Julius Shulman; 127 Timothy Hursley; 128, 129, 130 © Kim Jaen Yorn 132/3 APL; 134, 135T MEPL; 135B APL; 136 MEPL; 137 The Albuquerque Museum; 138, 139, 140, 141, 142/3 APL; 144, 145, 146 Balthazar Korab; 148T BAArch; 148B Hugh Pearman; 149 Lufthansa Archive; 150 Unique Airport, Zurich; 151 MEPL; 152, 153 APL; 154/5 Hugh Pearman; 156/157 APL; 158/159 © Paul Maurer; 162, 163T Peter Lewitt, Architectural Photography; 163B Esto/Bill Maris; 164.165 © Paul Maurer;168 Hugh Pearman; 169 Dennis Gilbert/View 176, 177, 178/9 Patrick Bingham-Hall; 181© Paul Ott, Graz; 183 Paolo Monello; 189T Albatross Aerial Photography, Tel Aviv; 191 Felix Gottwald Fluglotse2000@gmx.de; 192, 193 Duccio Malagamba; 194, 195 Hisao Suzuki; 198, 199t Timothy Hursley; 200,201 Jay Langlois; 203 Timothy Hursley; 204 © Simon Smithson; 206 APL; 207 Flight International; 208 © ADP; 209 © Paul Maurer; 216 Unique Airport, Zurich; 218, 219 Engelhardt/Sellin, Aschau; 220 Dennis Gilbert/View; 221, 222/3 Tomio Ohashi; 228, 229 Steinkamp/Ballogg; 231 Jay Berkowitz/Los Angeles World Airport